INNER BUSINESS

INNER BUSINESS

Training Your Mind for Leadership Success

Linda Björk

BALBOA
PRESS

A DIVISION OF HAY HOUSE

Balboa Press books may be ordered through booksellers or by contacting:

Balboa Press
A Division of Hay House
1663 Liberty Drive
Bloomington, IN 47403
www.balboapress.com
1 (877) 407-4847

Because of the dynamic nature of the Internet, any web addresses or links contained in this book may have changed since publication and may no longer be valid. The views expressed in this work are solely those of the author and do not necessarily reflect the views of the publisher, and the publisher hereby disclaims any responsibility for them.

The author of this book does not dispense medical advice or prescribe the use of any technique as a form of treatment for physical, emotional, or medical problems without the advice of a physician, either directly or indirectly. The intent of the author is only to offer information of a general nature to help you in your quest for emotional and spiritual well-being. In the event you use any of the information in this book for yourself, which is your constitutional right, the author and the publisher assume no responsibility for your actions.

Cover photograph by
Florence Montmare.

Print information available on the last page.

ISBN: 978-1-5043-5221-5 (sc)
ISBN: 978-1-5043-5223-9 (hc)
ISBN: 978-1-5043-5222-2 (e)

Library of Congress Control Number: 2016903352

Balboa Press rev. date: 03/31/2016

For Harley and Popcorn.

TABLE OF CONTENTS

PREFACE

You there. Yes you. Don't you have anything better to do right now than read?

Shouldn't you be working? Or doing something productive? Don't you have a budget to balance? Financials to review? A Facebook status to update? A language to learn? A meeting to plan? A team to manage? Do you think this "reading" nonsense is really necessary because, if you ask me, it's a total waste of time.

Oh, I see what you're doing. You're trying to get rid of me! Who am I, you ask? Why, I'm the guy who doesn't want you to read this book. (If you insist on reading it anyway, I'll be the one who makes you feel guilty about doing such an unproductive thing.) Some call me stress, which is cool enough I guess. I prefer to think about the thorn in your side that keeps you on your toes. That keeps you winning.

You and I? We've met countless times. Remember? You willingly invited me into your life around the time you started high school. And now you're reading a book that claims to help you manage me. Ha ha, well that's cute! You think you don't want me around anymore, but face it. You'd be lost without me. Think of everything I do for you. If it weren't for me, you'd be nothing, and you'd be nowhere. You need me. I've heard you say you thrive with me in your life. You've Tweeted about me in the middle of the night. I keep you awake at all hours, and you're bragging about it.

Look around you. There've been hundreds of books written about me, that's how important I am! There are also a million others that create more of me, so this book won't rid you of me any quicker than any of the others will. Besides. You want me around.

You're still reading. Why? What would you be without me? What would drive you to succeed? What would motivate you to work harder? To do better? To get more? I'm rather insulted that you have taken me for granted.

He (or she) who dies with the most stress wins. Isn't that how the saying goes?

Stop reading.

PART ONE

A primer in mind training

Progress is impossible without change and those who cannot change their minds cannot change anything.
—George Bernard Shaw

The NYC Subway Sneeze

It's a rainy spring morning in New York City (as many spring mornings here tend to be), and I'm taking my daughter to school.

I go to hail a cab, but my daughter pleads, "Mommy, can we take the subway?"

She looks up at me through the raindrops with her big eyes. Though I want to make the executive decision to get a cab, I remember her case of motion sickness on our last cab ride, so we make our way to the subway.

I pout all the way down to the subway platform on 66th Street. I check the train tracker. *Four* minutes! An eternity for any New Yorker. I continue pouting as I stand sternly on the platform, holding my daughter's hand. I think to myself how a cab would have been *so* much better.

The train finally arrives. Is it always this loud?

As we step into the car, someone sneezes big and wide.

Disgusting! We just got through winter, and I do *not* need us to catch whatever that sneeze is carrying. Gosh, people are annoying. Look at them! What are we even doing here, sharing our morning with virus-spreading machines on the subway? What an utterly uncivilized way to travel.

Let me pause the story here and tell you that I am a trained mindfulness instructor. I have had a daily meditation practice for nineteen years. During my ten years as the CEO of a creative agency in Stockholm and New York, I pioneered the use of mind training and mindfulness-based stress reduction techniques with my staff. These days, I lecture about awareness, the mind, what happens in the brain when we are under stress and, most importantly, what we can do to reach our own optimized version of self. I know very well that stressful thoughts produce hormones that compromise our immune systems.

In that moment, on the subway, I was not only an embarrassment to myself; I was at risk of catching a cold, or worse.

I shift my focus to the movement of the subway car. I remember the first time I took the subway to Brooklyn. It was two decades ago, also on the red line, and I was on my way to my first job at BAM. I had never set foot in Brooklyn before and I remember being petrified at every stop.

I smile and cringe as many oblivious "wide-eyed" moments on the subway flash before my eyes. Like the times I took the subway to JFK from Hells Kitchen and to La Guardia from Park Slope. Let's just say that the G-train twenty years ago was not a safe proposition. For anyone! Let alone for Scandinavian girls in mini-shorts with colorful suitcases going down to Miami Beach for the long-weekend. The subway was just brilliantly cheap. It's taken me everywhere.

I remember filming on the train to Coney Island, documenting the obscure observations made by a monochrome painter I assisted at the time. I snicker as I recall meditating on the B-train all those mornings in the 90s. I think about all the important meetings, dates, galas, classes and dinners I have used the subway to get to, as the above-ground reality of New York City has turned mad and congested.

I look at my daughter and smile widely as I think about that big BRIO stroller I schlepped around the city when she was a baby. Up and down the subway lines to get a hold of her special formula. The countless people who've lent a helping hand in the stairs. I squeeze my daughter's hand a little tighter.

I look around at the people in the subway car. Some of them seem to have been traveling far. Perhaps they are heading back home after a night shift? Or are they going to work? Visiting someone in the hospital? Catching a new break? I don't know. But wherever they're coming from and wherever they're going, they couldn't do it without the subway. Just like me and millions of other people, they depend on this subway system to make their lives work. From Far Rockaway Beach to 242nd Street…

The doors of the subway open. "Wow, we're already at 96th Street! Time to get off, Honey!"

We exit the subway car, and I'm convinced, knowing what I know about mind-body connections, that I have just saved myself from catching whatever virus was in the sneeze.

INTRODUCTION

The Speed of Stillness to Global Greatness

Although I have personally kept with a daily meditation practice most of my adult life, I never intentionally set out to use meditation as a tool for my employees. It started when I asked myself an important business-oriented question back in 2007, when I was still relatively new at being a CEO:

How can I prepare my staff to achieve global greatness?

As a CEO of a branding agency, I had already committed to my personal three-part vision. I was determined to crack the code that would:

- see our agency make great money
- have us create great work, and
- make us all feel great in the process.

I wanted our agency in Sweden to go global, and I needed the staff prepared for that to happen. I knew that an advanced business English class was not going to cut it; neither would enrolling in yet another management course. I needed something powerful—something that would make my staff fearless and creative. I needed them to be big thinkers, comfortable deal-makers and pleasant people.

What I needed was for them to meditate.

Yes, you read that right. Meditate. You might have a preconceived notion about meditation being reserved for hippies who don't believe in deodorant.

But as it happened, meditation would become one of the most important answers to my strategic question.

The New "It" For Business Success

So here's for a fun question: What do Oprah (no last name required), Russell Simmons and Arianna Huffington have in common?

How about NBA Legend Phil Jackson, Rapper 50 Cents and Congressman Tim Ryan?

They keep with a daily meditation practice.

And they are pretty busy people, which means that, if *they* can find time for meditation every day then so can you and I. (Bummer. No such excuse to hide behind. And we're only on the first few pages here!)

In the last couple of years, meditation as a means to reach a higher level of business success has made front-page news of one respected magazine after another. Meditation is truly a modern day "it" factor of success.

From my own business success as a CEO, I can personally attest to the remarkable effects of keeping with a meditation practice in the workplace. And my achievements are utterly modest in comparison to many impressive business leaders in the creative industry and beyond. Steve Jobs, Google engineers and the U.S. Army are diverse examples of global top-performers who've used meditation for stress-lowering and mind-expanding benefits. More and more companies are joining the movement that *Time* magazine calls "The Mindful Revolution." These companies, by the way, include Twitter, Apple, General Mills, Intel and Time Warner. CEOs of these companies understand the value in having employees with relaxed minds.

Ray Dalio is the founder of Bridgewater, the largest hedge fund firm in the U.S. This is a guy who has made his billion dollar fortune in one of the most high-pressured industries you can imagine. (Caveat: I am not saying that the stress levels in the financial sector are necessarily higher than the stress levels that a mid-western high-school teacher experiences. Stress is always relative to your own life, and stress is not choosy in who it visits and who it leaves in peace.)

Bridgewater is, however, the utmost symbol of modern power. It operates in the lions' den of a money-making machine, impacting the balance of the world economy. This is where things get interesting: The same guy who created this impressive power emporium from scratch is a committed advocate for meditation. Actually, Mr. Dalio credits meditation as the *biggest factor* for his success.

> *Meditation more than anything in my life*
> *was the biggest ingredient of whatever success I've had.*
> —Ray Dalio, billionaire Founder of Bridgewater,
> the world's largest hedge fund firm

When you start your meditation practice, you will discover, as Dalio did, that calming your mind and training yourself to be more in alignment with yourself—and possibly a higher creative force—invites success far beyond what you thought was possible. Mr. Dalio says that "meditation has given [him] centeredness and creativity" and that "it's also given [him] peace and health." These are no small words about meditation coming from the master of the universe of money-making.

The potential inside a higher functioning mind is still largely an unexplored corporate business development opportunity. Meditation—as a means to effectively handle stress, calm the mind, and expand our intelligence—is a sustainable way to increase your company's bottom-line, your workers' effectiveness and awareness, and everybody's wellbeing, as well as finding meaning and belonging.

The more I learn about the brain, the more I feel like shouting, "Help, somebody call somebody!" It's just crazy! There are certain parts of our brains that we need access to in order to figure things out, connect the dots, get a feel for people—you know; to be smart! If you think the brain is good to go as it is, think again.

First of all, left to its own devices, the brain is incapable of distinguishing be-tween real and perceived threats. So, we end up experiencing stress reactions from things that aren't actually happening and that prevents us from thinking clearly. It happens a bit like this: we think about something bad that could happen and we react with feelings of stress to that very thought and have ef-fectively impacted our brain and bodily system to believe we are in peril; our primitive amygdala lights up like a Christmas tree and dumps stress hor-mones through our bodies like a mean Santa Claus. It's like a big, red stress alarm button that gets pushed by the sheer work of our own thoughts and feelings. And here's another cruel joke: if the stress button is pushed in for too long, it gets stuck in emergency mode! But it doesn't stop there.

The brain apparently has a "narrative mode" set to default. Now, it would be nice to think that when we don't focus on anything in particular, the brain could enjoy some R&R. That it would kick back, relax a little, be calm, be quiet, and be still. No-sir-ee Bob. Instead of relaxing, it starts chattering away to itself like a deranged squirrel. By default! Didn't I tell you, somebody should call somebody! Too bad that both stress and mind-chatter make it so much harder for us to use the executive parts of our brains. You know. The magical place where everything from decision making and learning to emo-tional intelligence and intellect happen. Sigh.

This, my friend, is where meditation comes in. The brain's little super hero, helping to remove the blocks and speed bumps standing between you and your executive brain. Meditation and mindfulness, you see, have been proven to straight up make the amygdala smaller, ease up on our stress reaction alarm mode, and make it easier for us to, even in stressful situations, access our executive part of the brain.

> ***Where there is peace and meditation,***
> ***there is neither anxiety nor doubt.***
> —St. Francis de Sales

By now, meditation as an all-around wellness strategy for a company has been scientifically proven to increase your ability to focus, raise your aware-ness levels, and train you to keep calm under pressure. It's no wonder that it is so vital for business results and reaching creative heights. Meditation as a part of corporate culture really should be considered a possibility for any organization.

Not to say that implementing meditation into my organization wasn't always... ehm... easy. Some employees jumped at the opportunity of an eight-week mindfulness program, and others were, mildly put, dead against it.

Luckily, I was already considered weird and goofy, yet good at delivering results. A combination that bought me a little space with most skeptics. Still, I had two self-proclaimed non-starters. With a good argument, I would let them off the mindfulness hook. As much as it sucked, I concluded that I couldn't *force* my employees into self-development.

Nay-sayer One argued that the only objection he had was that he did not feel comfortable sharing personal information in a room with other employees, and, although no personal information needs to be shared in mindfulness, I could understand his point. I said fair enough, I will sign you up for an intensive mindfulness course for leaders instead, which he at that point couldn't turn down. I told him he could complain about it in hindsight though, which was an opportunity he couldn't resist. (BTW, knowing about the reality of how people function in the workplace is why I choose to mix my mindfulness teaching with hands-on mind-training tools. There are just too many escape hatches for our egos to prevent personal development if mindfulness is the only tool.)

Nay-sayer Two begrudgingly joined the lot of us for our weekly mindfulness course but sat with his arms sternly crossed over his chest the first couple of sessions. He then told me that it was ridiculous to call this mindfulness. *This is focus training!* he exclaimed. And from that day on, with him within earshot, I called it focus training. If a different name than "mindfulness" would make him show up, be open, and reap the rewards, I was all for it. I felt confident that results would unfold, whatever we called it.

Before we started taking care of our inner business at the agency, we had zero global accounts. When I decided to leave the company a few years (and many mind-training and meditation hours) later, we had five.

I told you, I like results.

The only real mystery is, why aren't all CEOs making meditation a part of their workday? Why aren't all companies making mindfulness and mind-training part of their culture? Don't they know?

> *The thing about meditation is:*
> *You become more and more you.*
> —David Lynch

This book is going to teach you how to not only awaken and embrace your own inner business (more about that in a minute), but it will also give you the tools you need to get your staff working mindfully, and helping you all to meet your personal and professional goals. Can you imagine knowing how to handle stress, how to get unstuck, be present and have your life working for you? Pretty great, yes? Now imagine everybody in your company knowing that same stuff.

I'm going to assume here for a minute that many of the concepts in this book are going to be unfamiliar to you, so let's get a few things straightened out.

What is Mindfulness?

Let's get it out of the way: mindfulness is not about Buddhism. It's not a promotion of Buddhism, and there are no political or religious affiliations around mindfulness. When we read about mindfulness and read about mindfulness research, we are mostly really reading about Mindfulness Based Stress Reduction, also known as MBSR.

MBSR was developed in the 1970s by Dr. Jon Kabat Zinn, a trained bio-molecular scientist from MIT, as an outpatient clinic for medical patients. MBSR is taught as an eight-week program and has been scientifically developed, tested, measured and tweaked to teach people how to pay attention. Relaxation, stress reduction, anxiety reduction, and a host of performance enhancements happen as a result of the practice, but in essence, it is about paying attention; in other words, about being aware and actually experiencing life.

Putting it in briefer terms: Mindfulness is the practice of non-judgmental awareness of the here and now. The present moment. The only moment there ever is.

Some people are able to be in a mindful state without seemingly having to do any work to live there. But for most of us, we need to practice a bit in order to get there. No wonder, as modern people, we are bombarded with information all the time (bring the smartphone to the john, anyone?), and we easily get caught up in thought patterns that clutter our capacity to use our brains effectively. We simply have too many thoughts, and they're all fighting for our attention.

> *Meditation is not a way of making the mind quiet. It's a way of entering into the quiet that's already there – buried under 50,000 thoughts the average person thinks every day.*
> —Deepak Chopra

For those of us who have to do a bit of work to live life in a calm, alert state—a mindful life if you will—well, we need to practice mindfulness exercises and mindfulness meditation. This is where we teach our minds how to simply pay attention, and we do so through our bodies, our breath, our senses, and anything else that arises in the moment.

As for some nuts and bolts of mindfulness, there are two types of mindfulness practice: formal and informal.

Formal mindfulness practice involves different meditations. Examples of formal mindfulness practice would be mindfulness yoga, walking meditation, body scan meditation, and breathing meditation. A bit of a meditation smorgasbord so that anyone can find a version that works with his or her life situation and character.

Informal mindfulness practice is when we pay full attention to activities that belong to our everyday lives. Like doing the dishes, brushing our teeth, listening to a friend, taking the stairs, drinking tea… just focusing on the activity in full presence. Nothing else.

When you train your mind through formal and informal meditation practices, you are literally rewiring your brain to do less mind-wandering. As your brain gets increasingly trained to focus on what matters, your so-called "thought clutter" dissolves. The process is a bit like going to the gym, minus the sweat and the questionable gym aesthetics. Every time your mind wanders in meditation and you "bring it back" to the present moment, you are effectively doing a bicep curl for your inner capacity to be present.

No matter how you slice the dice,
life is only available in the present moment.

When you can train your mind to "be with it" in presence, in attention and awareness, you're going to notice that life gets quite a bit easier and a lot more enjoyable.

As you adopt mindfulness in your life, you're choosing to adopt a non-judgmental awareness of the present moment. You're also choosing to adopt a few different attitudes. Specifically, there are nine of them. (I'll tell you what they are in a moment.)

As you begin to pay attention to these nine attitudes, you'll notice a real shift in your awareness. This not only bodes for a kinder and more joyful life, but you will benefit greatly in business. (*Finally! I thought she forgot that this is a business book! Let's get right to the WIFM and ROIs, why don't we?*). Respect man—it's the name of the game, and here we go:

- You'll stop wasting valuable time on unproductive thoughts.
- You'll be much sharper at cutting to the chase of what you want to accomplish.
- You'll spare yourself (and the company) destructive conflicts.
- You'll find yourself in a kinder and more cooperative atmosphere.
- You'll "level up" as a more aware leader with a more mature way of handling tasks.
- You'll become a more awake businessperson, with new eyes for new opportunities.
- You'll be far more creative, connecting new dots.
- You'll be able to inspire enthusiasm, creativity and innovation in others.
- You'll have a new compass to steer your company's health to meet its wealth.

So, what are these attitudes, you ask? Keep reading!

Attitudes in Mindfulness

1. Acceptance
2. Non-Judgment
3. Patience
4. Trust
5. Non-Striving
6. Beginner's Mind
7. Letting Go
8. Gratitude
9. Generosity

If you are rolling your eyes wondering what these things have to do with business development and leadership, I understand. It's easy to dismiss these values as yet another host of popular feel-good sound-bites floating around the internet. Or perhaps your mind drifts to Birkenstock-footed yoga teachers who couldn't spell profit if their lives depended on it.

My only pair of Birkenstocks, by the way, is adorned with Swarovski crystals, and I happen to *love* profits. These attitudes over the years have helped me up my level as a more aware leader and a more awake business person. Paying attention to each of these attitudes has allowed me to cut to the chase and stop wasting time on a lot of fruitless thoughts. I have seen opportunities where I was once blind. And vice versa. (Not blindness where there used to be opportunities—LOL—but I've recognized that some opportunities felt good based on the wrong things and were, in fact, dangers that should be avoided.) Big picture: these attitudes have helped me in my quest of having the company's health meet its wealth—while doing work that we are proud of. And, yes, I do feel a lot kinder these days, and, as per a huge coincidence, the world is much kinder to me.

For every section of this book, a couple of these mindfulness attitudes will be examined in relation to leading ourselves—our inner business and our outer businesses—to new, awesome heights.

GETTING YOUR INNER BUSINESS BACK

Imagine for a moment that you are running two businesses: an inner business and an outer business. Your inner business is being managed inside of you. It is the business of "being you"; the core of you; your heart, your truth, your emotional, mental and interconnected real you (here, needless to say, you are ideally the one calling the shots). And your outer business is the brick and mortar or service-based operation that you get paid to run (here, you may already be working hard to be calling the shots).

A true leader will manage the inner business as passionately as he or she would an outer business. And you know how to do the outer business already: You have a mission to meet, a vision for your business, and you are knowledgeable about your business and that which surrounds it. You develop a certain sensitivity for your business—you feel the trends and know the short-term deals and long-term consequences. You build a sustainable structure and find the right employee for each position, and you ensure that everything is running smoothly so that your company is serving you, your mission and your vision. But we aren't all leading our inner business with this kind of awareness—or meeting its basic requirements. On some level, though, we all know what happens with a business that is uncared for.

Unbeknownst to many of us, we are letting someone else (or something else) run our inner business. These unqualified team members start running the show as soon as (and as long as) we let them. And, not knowing better, we just step back and let them have their way. With *our* inner business! Somebody call somebody!

Take a deep breath.

As we'll take steps and leaps to get your inner business in better order, you will learn how to distinguish your intuition from your fear, excitement from panic, truth from ego, and a calm mind from an apathetic one. Not to mention how you, with your own inner business in order, can tell how someone else is doing with theirs. Oh, the money and heartache you'll save!

As you expand in your inner business, you will start to develop a natural inclination for feeling good on the inside and making the world a better place. (You noticed the order there, yes?) This happens as your inner knowing seeks ways to help and grow instead of unknowingly putting up barriers in the way of your dormant awesomeness.

This is an exciting proposition and one you obviously are ready for. Otherwise you wouldn't be reading this. Unless, of course, you were given this book at a costly seminar, and you feel obligated to read it. If it turns out that you really *are* bored to tears from spending time with yourself, this inner business stuff is guaranteed to feel like a uphill battle for you. But then again, if that's the case, chances are that you don't have such a blast with yourself when you're not getting to know yourself anyway, and that it's been a while since you had an exciting thought or, even a *new* thought entering your stratosphere. So, you might as well dive into your inner business with the rest of us.

Whatever walk has taken you here to this point, if you actually want to feel better about yourself, feel more confident in your contributions to your company, feel powerful as a business leader, and actually be in awe of how you are experiencing life… it is on your inside we need to start working.

A mind at war with itself
creates a world full of war.

Just think about the scientifically proven fact that virtually all of us replay the same thoughts, with the same accompanied feelings, day in and day out for most of our lives. And then we die. It's almost funny that we're all surprised that we're feeling tired and stuck! Good news for you: We will learn how to identify and stop these tedious repeat-thoughts and open ourselves up to more new experiences. We have lives to live!

Bigger Than Huge

There is now an overwhelming agreement in various scientific fields that all point to meditation and mindfulness to reach a deeper understanding and connection with oneself. These methods are proven to increase focus, reduce stress, calm the mind, heighten alertness, strengthen awareness, increase sleep quality, and control moods, as well as increase efficiency, wellbeing and happiness levels. Research on mindfulness and meditation is very specific in effects ranging from improved blood pressure to an actual increase of the brain's gray matter. It is tested as effective as medication for depression—without the side effects. The list is actually endless.

It is clear that meditation, with all its superior results in "soft" matters (basically everything that makes life worth living) also boasts a host of results that has to do with your intelligence (such as better memory and new brain cells). If you're pretending to be an unimpressed teenager right now with a p-p-p-p-poker face, I say silly goose! This is earth shattering!

And ta-da; These are the methods this book is based on.

As a business proposition, this is huge.

As a life proposition, this is even bigger. And we like bigger than huge.

Our minds are our least explored business development areas, with the highest potential for extraordinary growth.

When we master the ability to keep our minds calm in any given situation and we learn how to be much more alert and open to possibilities around us, there is really no limit to what we can achieve. When we meditate in an effective manner, we train our minds to do these very things. We go way beyond learning management methods for each and every situation we may encounter. We go deeper than trying to change our attitudes. We go beyond the psychology of looking back at childhood traumas that impact our behaviors.

When meditation is effective, it deeply relaxes our nervous-system—even deeper than a good night's sleep. A meditative state creates calm in the very bottom of our being where our fears, without any doing, can dissolve.

Sounds fantastic, does it not?

But there are some things standing in the way of our optimized lives in mindfulness—things preventing us from getting a proper handle on our inner business. The number one thing to address is named Mr. Stress. And before we get to know him better, let me just say that the really sneaky thing about stress is that the long-term detrimental effects of stress don't set off any alarms of our stress response system. If it did, we'd stop stressing immediately, no questions asked. But it doesn't, so the same mechanism can just continue and nothing says Stop! If you let that sink in, you'll recognize it for what it is: the most brilliant conspiracy theory to date. We need to smarten up, CIA style.

Mr. Stress

Meet Mr. Stress, the modern day beast we freely allow into our living spaces. (You heard from him before. He even wrote the preface to this book.)

Mr. Stress promises he'll help us get more things done in less time while he whispers sweet words of an exhilarating life in the fast-lane. His presence is easily recognized as it comes with a slight to severe sensation in the pit of our stomach, accompanied by the nagging idea that we are not good enough if we don't do more.

Most of us invite him willingly into every room and situation of our lives. Stress is like Dr. Jekyl and Mr. Hyde with a health-veto. We all know that he is really bad for us, yet we can't seem to help ourselves. Dr. Jekyl is kind of exciting and so helpful… and we need him in order to be successful, right?

I thrive on stress! I do better when I am stressed!

Stress lures us in with the idea that *of course you have to do more and do it faster*. When things pile up and we become a drill sergeant version of ourselves, we get a kick out of being the one who can juggle more balls than humanly possible—in record time, too! We are drawn to push ourselves, meet impossible deadlines, and, if we just manage to squeeze in a little more into our crammed schedule (perhaps even impressing our clients and Twitter followers with our all-nighters), we feel even better about our super qualities. The world would stop moving without us! No, seriously, it would! Our stress is powering the big hamster wheel at the center of the universe!

When we react with stress, we ask our bodies for a bionic boost. We demand our bodies to be pushed even harder, and (ta-daa) our human bodies come with a natural mechanism to comply. We release stress hormones with cortisone and adrenaline. For a while, we are on turbo charge.

Our natural reaction to stress is a highly useful function as it helps us survive temporary hardships. Think of it as our bodies going on natural steroids to deal with these sudden and horrific threats. This awesome trump card that kicks in with our so-called flight-fight-freeze response is here to increase our chances of survival. We can run faster, we get physically stronger, and we even bleed less if we are injured during a stressful episode.

Historically, it probably went down like this:

Intruder in cave − scared response − run or beat intruder with stick.

Big brown bear − scared shitless response − run or play dead.

It makes perfect sense that this is a built-in "add-on" that comes with all models of human beings. But as all car lovers know, it's the add-ons that get you.

This stress-response mechanism that is meant to save us *temporarily* has become the biggest double-edged sword in modern times. We want to run faster and be stronger *all the time*.

The human body can only react heroically to stress for so long. Yet, most of us are raising the stress bar for what we should be able to handle. The more we think we can handle, the higher we raise the bar. "What? I just pulled two all-nighters, won the pitch, and now I'm pushing 80-hour weeks to meet the deadline—sure I can do that again! In fact, I'll draw up next year's budget on that speed, and we'll make great profits!"

We make our life calculations based on these naturally induced steroid episodes thinking that this is what we should be able to handle. But there is, of course, one big rub. We are *gasp* human beings (Shucks!). And, as much as we are constructed to *temporarily* react to stressful situations with bionic strength, thanks to chemicals and hormones, those very same chemicals and hormones will kill us. No kidding. These chemicals, given some time, will break our system down from the inside. We are literally poisoning our own bodies with stress.

So now you have heard it again: stress is detrimental to your health.

Stress has been coined the biggest contributing factor for most illnesses in the western world. In other words, no other single factor will make you as seriously sick as much as stress. Stress causes more illnesses than smoking! If you smoke today, you are basically a ticking time bomb, guaranteed to get cancer. Yet, we're all stressing out like it's going out of style.

Although overwhelming stress doesn't have to be here to stay, having a lot on our plates will probably never cease to be reality for many of us. We have to understand how we can continue living our high-level lives while significantly reducing our stress levels. Much like any other self-invited guest, asking Mr. Stress to leave takes some finagling.

Stress is the unyielding wedge between you and your greatest potential for health, wealth and happiness.

As a CEO, before I became a Mindfulness Instructor, I had little respect for the effects of stress and, especially, burnouts. It's kind of terrible for a boss to admit, but I thought people should just shape up and not be so sensitive about everything. *Come to work! Perform! Go home! How hard can it be?*

Well, as it happens, it's very hard to do much of anything once you have burnt the nerve-threads in your brain. New research actually shows that burnout can leave permanent brain damage. (Whoops!)

As I began to realize that I was doing physical damage to myself (and the people working for me), with my CEO tail dragging between my legs, I started looking for a better solution than my previous over-achiever attitude. Simply put, it was time to take Mr. Stress seriously.

In my research, I've found that it is not the actual *workload* per se that makes most people reach a point of burn out. It's their inability to find a healthy emotional response to the work demands—either by setting healthy boundaries as to what's humanly possible to deliver (e.g., saying no) or by developing mental capacities to deal with stressful thoughts and feelings of overwhelm.

In other words, people's *worry* about anything in relation to their workload is the real catalyst for burnout.

As it relates to work, we worry about not being appreciated, not being good enough, and disappointing others. These are factors that are alarmingly important to us. Throw an unrealistic workload on top of this messy mental state, and we're in a lethal catch 22. Not only are we sleep deprived and mentally drained, but we also feel like we're never going to be good enough or that we ever do enough. And there we are, too overwhelmed to deal with our negative mental state that set us off not being able to handle the overwhelming workload in the first place.

Other research has found that fewer than one in three Americans receive praise from their work supervisor (!) and employees who say they have not been recognized at work are more likely to quit in the next year. Add to that the vast amount of physical and psychological damage stress causes, and you know where the countless days of sick leave and staff turnarounds come from.

This sounds expensive, no? (All business managers nod.)

As I've dug deeper into my research, it's become clear to me that the issue of stress goes way beyond workload and worry.

There is something larger at play.

When we drill deeper down into our beings, we find that we're frantically running around doing things we aren't meant to be doing in this life. And though it sounds a little lofty, we can often feel it. We feel "off course" when our actions and contributions in life don't match up with what we feel we really should be doing or company values we really feel we should be supporting. That's a lot of running around in the wrong direction. No wonder we're feeling stressed and ill at ease.

We may even feel quite the severe discord in ourselves because we are playing too small. To settle for a life meant for someone else brings enormous stress to our systems. We are not living our authentic lives, and we feel it.

Perhaps we're more sensitive than we thought to what our *true selves* really want for us.

Perhaps we get stressed because we don't focus on what is really important. Instead, we spend massive amounts of energy sweating things that, after closer examination, mean little to us. Some of us are reaching a point where we simply can't outrun ourselves anymore. We need to find a new level in our work, our careers, our lives—one that resonates with who we really are and uses the full force of our natural powers.

I know for sure that there is no coincidence that we are where we are. I also know that it is impossible to be in the present moment while you are stressed out and that it is impossible to truly feel alive when you are overwhelmed. I also know for sure that once you learn to be in alignment with yourself, you can stop the worry-overwhelm cycle and discover who you really are and what you are meant to do here.

This "getting to know yourself stuff" might smell a little too much like a New Age book to you, which, in turn, feels like the worst possible antidote to your challenging business reality.

You may be thinking something along these lines:

It's impossible to have my job and not be stressed out. That's the whole idea! And I don't want to quit my job. I won't be able to make this kind of money anywhere else. I don't want to join a meditation commune, sing kum-ba-ya and grow my own vegetables—and I sure as hell don't want to let my armpit hair grow long! I like my fancy shoes and trips to the Bahamas, thank you very much.

Our minds do that to us. They take one emotional queue and run off with it. As with many exhausting mind-threads, this one doesn't have much merit to it at all. Except, perhaps, observing how easily the mind spins out of control in a worst-case-scenario cycle of thoughts and emotions. This effectively shuts your brain down, preventing new ideas from entering.

This mind spin thing happens in business all too often, resulting in many missed business opportunities.

That's why having a calm, clear mind is the only effective way to make good, sound decisions.

That's why being in alignment with yourself is necessary for knowing what your vision really is.

That's why knowing who you are is a prerequisite for being a great leader.

Getting to know yourself, learning how to be in alignment with yourself, and mastering how to have a non-stressed mind even in the most dire of circumstances will take some practice. And don't worry—we can practice far away from a New Age bookstore. (Though maybe we should examine why New Age books make you nervous.)

Rest assured, you can grow an aware, clear, calm mind and still continue in the same position or career you have right now—if that's what you want. The difference is, you will know how to use your mental capacities for feeling much better and growing your business—and yourself—beyond what you ever dared imagine.

If you decide not to be in the same job as a result of becoming a more mature person with an expanded intelligence, then I'm sure whatever you end up doing will outshine your current position. You have nothing to fear from growing. But let's not get ahead of ourselves. This we know right now: You are in business. You want to excel. A lot of things are stressing you out.

Let's start here.

You Are The Boss

Now that we have turned our attention to what matters the most in how you perceive life and feel about your life (i.e., your inner business, what constitutes being you), we will have quite a few things to talk about.

I want you to be as wise, swift and sustainable with your inner business as you may already be (or at least dream of being) with your outer business—and then we'll see how your inner changes will reflect in your outer reality. No matter how successful you are with your outer business, it will mean nothing if your inner business feels like hell.

When we've gone through the lot of how to build a ship-shape inner business, I still want you to remember the number one priority in having your inner business in order: knowing how to handle stress. If you can't handle stress, there isn't much growth in other areas to be had.

We will briefly go over the positive sides of stress and how to use them. Truth of the matter is, however, that having too little stress in life is not a problem many of us face. Hence, the focus on stress in this book will be how to befriend and lessen the damaging, overwhelming kind of stress that is getting the best of most of us.

Imagine that Mr. Stress is working for you in your inner business—the business you need to manage and master. You would manage Mr. Stress just like you would anyone else. Except, Mr. Stress is one of those employees you can't fire and can't send to another company location. You're stuck with him. Much like having employees in Sweden.

Time to open up to the good news:
You are the boss of your inner business.

You may not have felt that you are the boss of your inner business thus far, but I'm here to tell you: You are the chief commander of you. By the virtue of being who he is, Mr. Stress will always try to take your executive position of power. But you won't let him, now that you'll be smarter than he is sneaky. You will find a position suitable for him, like you do with any employee, in a structure that ultimately benefits the business (e.g., you!).

Knowing that your inner business is your business, you can now look at it with vision and care, like you would with any outer business that you run.

You will define your mission, know your purpose, and make sure to gain tools in your business that serve you.

The slight difference will be that you're probably not accustomed to running your outer business with a long-term strategy where the exit-plan means that you are... ehm... no longer around, but that's what you will learn with your inner business. This is your life. There are no rehearsals and no do-overs. As you shift towards taking care of your inner business, you will see that your inner business is here to serve your outer business... not the other way around.

My wild guess (because it's true for the vast majority of everyone) is that Mr. Stress is currently running your inner business. That you are not, in fact, in charge. As such, Mr. Stress is an unqualified leader who has taken over your company. And you're sitting back and letting him.

Not for long.

Leadership Pretzel No More

As ambitious leaders, you and I have a lot in common.

We've read miles upon miles of books to help us improve our performance and, more importantly, the collective performance of our teams.

We've attended (more than) our fair share of leadership seminars, management kick-offs and coaching courses. We've been taught methods and comebacks, strategies and value words.

The truth is, we've read more about what it takes to be great leaders than we care to remember.

All of these words of wisdom swirl in our over-stuffed brains: integrity, humility, credibility and authenticity, oh my!

You need to be the commander in control who delegates with determination. No. You need to be able to delegate *and* provide coaching and guidance! You must motivate your teams to greatness! No. You must inspire them to even greater greatness!

You must show them you trust them in order to earn their trust. Trust is the most important ingredient! No. Performance is. You have to perform! No, enthusiasm is. You have to be the enthusiast! No, equality is. No, having fun is. No, actually, it's all about innovation and creativity!

Always be accessible!

Take time for yourself!

Make sure you know the most!

Be humble and embrace what you don't know!

Achieve work/life balance!

Forget about work/life balance!

Hire up! Be in charge! Get out of the way! Roll up your sleeves! Be in a good mood! Be your best! Be fabulous! Be the most fabulous!

Ehrm... great.

Most of us have been through at least one of "those" leadership training programs that lift everyone's spirits for that afternoon only to have a bucket of good intentions fizzle into nothingness within a day or two.

No wonder. How can we expect a short-term influx of temporary intellectual information to make a lasting impact on our leadership skills? Leadership really does run deeper than that.

**As a business leader, you are invited to ask
the most profound questions in life.
Business asks: "Why are you here?"
Leadership asks: "Who are you?"**

Leadership opens the door to getting to know yourself and learning how to connect with other people on a deep, meaningful level.

In order to make a company or organization succeed beyond imagination, a great deal of hard work and strong leadership is required. Success does not happen in a glitzy happenstance; yet, everyone seeks a quick fix.

If you're like most of us in Corporate America, your primary business development efforts are likely focused on increasing profits. You're working all the time, and, yet, you're naggingly unfulfilled.

When we're unfulfilled, we tend to work harder.

Something's not right! We must grow faster! We need to get bigger! We need to work harder! But the nagging feeling of nonfulfillment is always there. We're using more force for more productivity in more markets, while not really getting a true sense of satisfaction. This is a frustrating equation guaranteed to catch up with anyone.

We run so fast that we've become blind to the fact that running fast in the wrong direction will not take us where we truly want to go.

**If "more, faster and harder" is not the answer,
then what's the secret to excelling as business leaders?**

Simply reading a few leadership books obviously isn't enough for leadership success.

To what or whom should we actually listen in order to become the great leaders we're yearning to be?

The answer is going to surprise you because I'm going to tell you that you shouldn't, first and foremost, listen to me, your partner, your president or your minister. And your parents' advice shouldn't take presidency either. So who should you listen to, first and foremost? Yourself.

Listening is an art that requires practice.
Listening to yourself is a mastery that takes skill.

Here's an expanded version of that answer: As long as you don't know how to skillfully run your inner business, the "you" you're listening to is not going to be helpful. Together, we will get to know the different decision makers in you that you need to be aware of and know how to handle and manage. As we do so, we will open up for you to get to know yourself and your true purpose.

After all, how can we expect to feel conviction about anything if we don't know who we are?

How can we reach a state of awareness if we keep running an ego-race?

How can we experience our own integrity if we are too stressed out to even reflect on what is important to us?

How do we ever get in alignment with our vision if we don't know our true purpose?

When you start asking yourself questions like these, the exploration and mastery of your inner business begins.

Your inner business has to be in order before you can enjoy and create an outer business flow. As you experience this, it will be evident how they effortlessly flow together.

As you get to know, organize, heal, and expand your inner business, you're in for a rich, colorful journey. The paradoxes and challenges will be many, and so will the doubts about the road traveled so far.

At this point, you're probably wondering whether this inner business stuff is even worth spending time on. And I know what you're thinking. *Jeez, this sounds like so much work! How much time is this actually going to take?*

Well, answering that question would be like answering, "how long does it take to explore life?" or "how long is a string?"

What you should be asking is: Will this inner business exploration make me grow? Will I have fun? Will I feel good? Will I use my life for something meaningful? Will I be happier? (The answer to all of those questions, by the way, is yes!)

> **Spending time getting to know yourself to a point where you can separate your gut-feeling from a gassy stomach really should be viewed as a useful proposition.**

Now, let's dive a bit deeper into this inner business stuff, shall we?

You vs. Business

Business brings a highly interesting paradox to your existence.

Naturally, you are a unique person, most likely with a unique soul, and most definitely with your own need of authentically expressing yourself to feel that you are truly alive. Business, on the other hand, is constructed for you to conform to a non-personal structure, to something that you are not.

Experiencing this paradox can be devastating. The inner battle of who you *are* versus who you are *expected to be* can lead to frustration, anger and depression. You may find yourself only occasionally in this devastating state—sometimes in a foul mood without even knowing why—or you may be living your life never feeling truly alive or whole.

It was quite the shock that slowly imploded in me as I started working in Corporate America. Bit by bit, my personal expression was taken away, and, with it, the core of my talent. We are asked to shut up and observe. *This is how things are done here. This is how we dress here. This is how we express ourselves here. This is how we greet each other here. This is the real pecking order here. This is how we ask things here. This is when we speak.* And between all the lines, *this is what we don't do here.*

How things are "being done here" is really saying, "this is our culture." Problem is, few companies have a thought-through business culture that allows for personal expression and cultural differences. In the process, we miss out on what makes everyone great: people's inherent power and system of intelligence that work so well in a person who doesn't have to be on guard for office politics. Of all the reasons I left Corporate America, frequently feeling underestimated of how I could contribute is high on the list.

> *To be yourself in a world that is*
> *constantly trying to make you something else*
> *is the greatest accomplishment.*
> —Ralph Waldo Emerson

The inner knowing that arises from a calm mind will help you navigate this inherent contradiction between Business (what you do and what you have) and the Natural You (who you really are and how you connect to everyone else).

The more you align your actions in the world with who you are,
what you believe to be true, and what makes you feel alive,
the more your life will work for you.

How do we know that? Because we can feel it, and we have observed it many times. When we are connected to an exciting idea, we feel like we are "on a roll" and, just like that, people and events seem to line up to support us. This alignment with yourself is what will solve the puzzle of how you can live fully while being in business—and see your business develop fully.

Did I mention that this whole "growing into fully living and expanding your mind and your business" thing will take some work on your part? Good. Because thinking that all of your problems will solve themselves simply by you reading these words would just not be accurate.

Mind-training certainly requires work. Meditation is called a practice because it requires consistent practice.

I call this process growing our inner business because, as with any business, we need to tend to our inner selves in order to make things happen and make ourselves—and that around us—grow.

Much like it takes many hours of crunches, planks and sit ups to bring great function and beautiful definition to our tummies, we need to work on toning our inner strength as well. As unfair as it may sound, there are some people out there who were born with six-pack abs without ever (literally) lifting a muscle, much like there are people who just seem to be happy, content and successful no matter what life throws their way.

Most of us, however, need to (sometimes begrudgingly) put in work to get ourselves into shape. Both at the outer (physical) and inner (mental) gym. But, as most healthy people know, the crunches and exercises are important for certain results, but nothing is as vital as an overall healthy lifestyle. The same thing goes for our inner mind mastery, where it all needs to start. Technically, you can use meditation methods to lower your stress while you continue making money from cheating the elderly out of their lifesavings. Great, you might think, now I'll have even more stamina for my thievery! But few would disagree that this would completely defeat the purpose. A skilled mind sees the power in kindness. A trained mind finds clarity in peace.

By now, I hope you're convinced that taking care of your inner business through meditation and mind-training is going to be a good thing for you. If we can align you and the world in one awesome flow, we're really onto something here, wouldn't you say?

But before we really dig into the meat of the program, we have to go over the rules. Luckily, there's only one.

The One and Only Rule

With this book, I invite you to explore the inner possibilities of your mind—what ways best suit you to significantly lower your stress levels, how you can use mind-training that applies to your specific business expansion, and how becoming aware is key for your personal growth.

I have written this to be purposely free of rules and must-dos. There are no definite answers other than the ones you will find to be true within yourself. Except... well... there *is* one rule:

You are not allowed to blame anyone for anything.

You actually have to stop doing that right now.

Blaming someone is an automated response for most of us. We see something broken or failed and the *first thing* that comes to mind is "Who did this?" rather than "How can we fix this?" And if it's broken beyond repair, which of course could be labeled unfortunate, it still is what it is. It can't be undone. No sense in playing the blame game.

Our inclination to blame stops us dead in our tracks in developing our minds and expanding our leadership. And, if you belong to the "blame yourself for everything" group, you are not doing any better. Blame strips your ability to grow, and self-defeating thoughts obliterate your power, so you cut it out, too!

From now on, every time you are inclined to blame someone, please observe yourself. Initially, you may go ahead and point the blame finger anyway, but now at least you will see it. And before you know it, you will see it before it is pointed—which will give you the opportunity to stop yourself, regain your power and get aligned with your true capabilities.

We will circle back to the importance for leaders to take ownership of everything that is happening later on in the book, but for now, start observing yourself in any situation that ignites your blame-response. If you want to find out what happened in a situation in order for you to prevent another incident from happening again, that's fine. But no blaming. That's the only rule in this no-blame game. And now, let's get on with the show.

PART TWO

The juicy stuff

The **INNER BUSINESS** Program

As we begin building our inner business to its intended glory, many of us start at a point of feeling stuck, overwhelmed, unappreciated, powerless and tired. Or perhaps you're just freakin' frustrated and that's all you know life to feel like. (Sad face.)

Behold, because the inner business program is arching over a few vital steps to finally land you in a position of power to inspire change. This is where you feel like yourself while having access to your inherent strength. You can be at peace on the inside, regardless of circumstance. This, my friend, is where you feel free.

I know, I know. I sense a few skeptical eyebrows rising, as the proposition is so grand. *That can't be true! Feeling like myself, feeling at peace and still being happy with my results in life? Really?*

Yes, really. And this will be made possible by exploring four major areas together. You and I... and you. Did I just say "you" twice? Yes. But I'm getting ahead of myself. The fact that there are more of you than you inside you is for later.

Here are the inner business areas, also formed as main chapters for **"Part II - The Juicy Stuff"** of this book:

1. BEING
2. FOCUS
3. POWER
4. SPARK

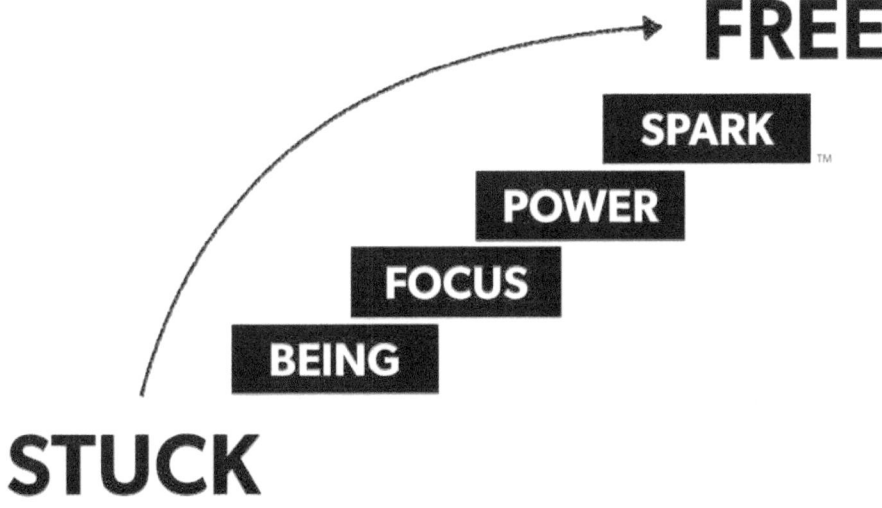

Ready to get started? Great. Let's go!

My Own Leadership Failure

Back in the day, as an up-and-coming leader with a position as a Creative Director in Corporate America, I was, mildly put, frustrated with the power struggles at play. I had people assigned to me who weren't as interested as I was in getting the work done and, even less so, in doing that work well. Although my cultural programming was one of inclusiveness, consensus and avoiding confrontation, I was completely swept up by the pressures and ruling culture around me.

I blush severely from inner embarrassment when I recall answering "because I told you so" to the questions of frustrated employees. And when things felt desperate and confrontational, I even recall saying, "do I have to remind you that it's actually your job to do what I tell you to do?"

I felt like a mental and emotional nightmare in high heels!

In the self-reflecting conversations with myself that followed, I defended myself, explaining that these people were male chauvinist bullies anyway, and there was really nothing I could have done differently. But the situations drained me—I didn't feel good, I didn't feel like myself, and my work suffered.

I finally realized that it actually didn't matter if these draining situations were provoked by someone else's behavior. No wonder I was feeling frustrated— by letting their behavior control me, I didn't feel free.

**In knowing what you don't want, what you truly desire
can be defined—and allowed to emerge.**

As I heard myself uttering sound bites against my own beliefs and my own sense of how I want to act in the world, I reached a turning point. I realized I had to be my own leader, on the inside of me. Even though I couldn't define it at the time, I felt the sensation of being able to observe myself from the inside. Something in me could observe something else in me. Today, I can see clearly how my "hobby" of daily meditation had granted me some inner space—what mindfulness calls "the gap"—enough so that I could bring awareness to a situation that I disagreed with (even though I was the one who had created it).

At some point in our lives, we all face situations where we have to step up and be the leader. This can happen in the big (when the building is on fire and you make sure everyone gets out safely) and in the small (when you help a friend see the brighter side of a seemingly dark situation). If nothing else, we all have our own lives to lead, and, as such, we are all leaders.

However, in situations where many people need to be orchestrated to achieve goals on a timeline, it becomes pretty clear that not everyone is holding the leadership stick. In most rooms, even far from corporate power structures, an informal pyramid of power quickly forms. So, who makes the real leader?

Most of us would agree that a leader who constantly has to prove her status is not a real leader. She might be the boss, but she is not a leader. It can be hard to intellectually distinguish a real leader from a power-induced boss, but we all feel the difference. We know when we meet someone who embodies the qualities of a leader, someone who simply *is* a leader. That's the real leader, title or no title.

So, yes, this "being stuff" is an abstract notion, but let's examine what this really means for your quest in being successful in your own leadership role.

**It is in the being of leadership that you will
find your true status, not in your title.
And not by being tall.**

As a leader, you will always be well served by people who identify you as a leader rather than fear you for your position of power. So, where do you find your true leadership?

To think that the answer is so within reach: You will find it in your own presence. This presence, in turn, will extend with a mental space, an emotional maturity and aware actions as a leader.

I'm sure you're action-oriented. Leaders generally are. But let's not put the cart before the horse. Your actions, albeit important, do not come first. Any actions that are *not* generated from awareness are potentially harmful—not only to yourself, but also to your staff, the company and the world.

The right kind of action will naturally arise from your presence, the only place you can tap into awareness and align with your very being as a leader.

> *The privilege of a lifetime is being who you are.*
> —Joseph Campbell

So, without further ado, let's explore both leadership and presence together, so that you can step into the *being* of a great leader.

The Antithesis of Being A Great Leader

As much as I cringe when I think of my own non-leadership moments in my career, I am so grateful that they happened. By experiencing what I didn't want, I had the opportunity to understand what bothered me. This allowed me to move forward with new information.

Here are some of the invaluable lessons that I learned from these frustrating and embarrassing situations:

- When I think I am controlling people, they are, in fact, controlling me.
- I can't control people; however, my own reactions to people are mine to control.

- I can't force anyone to greatness, but I can aspire to inspire a few.

What I did not realize in those early days was that I held my being in a reactive state. In other words, I was reacting to other people's words and actions rather than proactively approaching my work reality with a deeper sense of self. Victims live in a reactive state; victorious leaders live in the opposite. Because of this reactive state, I was easily frustrated.

> ### *Victims are dangerous people.*
> —Byron Katie

Even though I practiced meditation in my personal life, it was as if I left my open mind at home with my meditation pillow. As I drove to work, I added a layer of armor for every car I passed.

At the time, I did not know that the same thing that made me a great person would serve me the best as a leader. And the confines of the corporate culture certainly didn't help me to see that either.

Being Wanted

In later years, as the CEO of a creative agency, my insight about what constituted a true leader deepened. With several offices under my belt, I needed these separate units to work efficiently in my absence. In lieu of having myself cloned (I'm sure you can relate), I needed those who worked for me to perform as real leaders, and I needed them yesterday.

All that I'd been learning about leadership was going to have to be passed on to my people, such as the importance of checking your ego at the door, listening more than you speak, listening to other people beyond what they are saying in words, leading by example, and being mindful of how your energy impacts a room. Oh, and to never hover. People really hate that.

That sounded doable.

But what I hadn't factored in was the time it takes for emerging leaders to make their own mistakes. And I was in too much of a hurry to allow them to do so. My "do this and do that" instructions didn't do the trick. Of course! There are so many intricacies of skillful leadership, so many combinations of factors that makes a group accepting of you as the leader, that, again, the answer will be in the *being* of a leader rather than the doing. We need to learn how to align with some really abstract factors to make it work. Leadership is far from a mechanical endeavor. From all the trials and errors, it turned out that the most valuable instruction from me to the leaders was:

Your aim is for people to <u>want</u> you in the room.

The emerging leaders took the same route as I had taken in my earlier leadership years, which was to think that leadership was something you needed to stake. My flag is in the ground; therefore, I am the leader! This was evident as reports started trickling in from employees who were frustrated that many project discussions turned into arguments where the nail in the coffin was "well, I am the boss here now, so you have to run with what I'm saying."

And boy did I recognize that sentiment.

We were back to the concept of power-induced bosses. It was easy from my vantage point to see, yet again, that leadership happens in the *being* of leadership, definitely not in the staking of the power flag. Now it was my job to get them to *being*.

"The Way to do is to be."
—Lao Tzu

I asked these emerging leaders to assume a new north-star: For every meeting they were in, they were to ask themselves, "Am I wanted and/or needed in this situation?" If the answer was no, they had no reason to be there. If they were not helpful, they had to leave.

From a bigger perspective, what I was really doing with my staff was introducing them to the most transformative shift I had made in my own career, which was to ask the question: *How can I serve?*

You see, I had had it wrong for so long.

I thought climbing the ranks made me more important, with a bigger right to entitlement and deserving of more respect and rewards. Sure, my hourly rates were a lot higher than a junior, and menial tasks needed to get off my desk as soon as possible. That's simply good business. Sure, we all had different roles—everyone was responsible for their respective piece that together made up this big puzzle called our business.

When I talk about serving as a leader, I am not talking about doing the Starbucks runs and cleaning up the bathrooms. I am talking about an attitude of service. A deeper insight of realizing that, as a leader, the more you climb, the bigger your executive domains grow, and the more opportunities you have to make a positive impact in this world. And, as we know by now, it does not start with the big outer gesture of doing; it starts with the inner attitude towards being—recognizing that you are plenty in a room just by being you.

By constantly asking myself how I best can be of service in the situation before me is what ultimately turned my career into my vocation. Remember, your *true self* is always your first line of business and the first for you to serve. [Take a breath.] You have heard it before, and I am here to remind you: You cannot help others unless you have helped yourself.

Here is the "How to help others" list, broken down step by step:

1. Help yourself.
2. Help others.

If you are a container, you share *that which is spilling over* with other people. So, let's get working on filling you up with the greatness within. You have a job to do, way beyond your title.

The Leader Shift

When I truly started to experience the sweet spot between how I can serve and what I truly felt I was here to do, my love for leadership fully blossomed.

There is nothing wrong with striving to have success and prosperity, just as long as the path you choose does not require the shedding of your truth or joy or soul.
—Brendon Burchard

In order for you to be a desirable leader, to really be *wanted* as a leader, you need to contribute on several leadership levels.

Simply put: if you don't contribute as a leader, there is no reason for you to be there in that role. Your contribution as a good strategist, designer, sales person, or analyst is not what will make your contribution ultimately count as a leader. You may very well come up with the best idea to solve a situation and move forward, but it is key to remember that your opinions are not necessarily better just because you have a managerial or leadership title. In fact, your contribution as a real leader is *better* spent encouraging other people to come up with *their* best ideas. (Do I see a lightbulb turning on?)

On a deeper level, your biggest job is to make people who work around you feel seen and heard.

Being seen and heard for who we really are is one of the strongest longings we have, and is, therefore, one of the most powerful drives you can tap into with the human capital you want to see perform. It really is that easy with many employees.

I can still remember one of the biggest energy shifts I have ever experienced take place in my own office. One of my designers had under-performed for a while and had assumed a lackluster attitude including showing up late and smelling of yesterday's party drinks. I called him into my office and just breathed with him for a bit. I wanted him to feel that, although he may had been expecting reprimanding for his rather obvious misbehavior, he was safe with me.

After a while, I asked him sincerely *how are you doing?* He said *fine* and wanted to know why I asked. So I told him what I had observed. I chose to be quite specific with timing of events, my impressions of him, and the downward shape of his curve. This is when the energy-shift happened. This muted man with what seemed to be an undiagnosed depression was suddenly shining brighter than the sun, right there in my office. Why? Because I had seen him. He even said as much. He was so grateful to have been seen. He didn't think, because I'm a busy leader with my own office and all, that I had any idea what was going on with him or even perhaps cared. He was dumbfounded. His deepest need had been met. As a result, he completely turned the page. For the remainder of my time at the agency, he was not only a top-performing designer, but he also stepped into a leadership role of helping other designers shine.

This is why authenticity is a conclusive factor in being a great leader—the more you get seen and heard for who you really are, the easier you access the powerful sources within you. Why wouldn't someone do their very best for you, if you meet the needs they most long for?

Being Helpful

Here are a few different leadership levels where your contributions will be valuable and your presence wanted. Keep in mind that any act of competition or comparison from you can trigger other people's egos (more about ego in a little while). For now, let's just agree that it's a good idea to steer clear from provoking egos.

Keep your mind calm, your heart open, and your sights set on being helpful.

Here we go:

1. **Visionary** – Where is the group aiming? The perfect contribution from a leader is to help with the big picture. We all know how much valuable time is wasted in meetings, so take on the role of ensuring that this valuable time will lead somewhere useful. Perhaps you sense they're missing overarching values or goals in their process. Perhaps you see details that will steer them straight. But wait with your own opinions until you have given everyone a chance to reflect back their vision to you. That way, you start with a non-confrontational connection that opens up for further dialog and further contribution.

2. **Practically** – Can you do anything to help the group? Are there resources lacking? Do they need more data? Asking if the group needs anything takes no effort on your part, but the rewards are remarkable. Perhaps you have much easier access to information that would help their work process tremendously. Don't underestimate the power of making sure that the physical needs of staff are met—if you can provide them with the resources they need to succeed, you put real threads in your connection, you make the results come out better, and you show yourself to be a real leader. And please don't read this as tip-toeing for your teams. Showing a level of care that makes them feel seen while giving them tangible evidence that the company cares for them is just smart leadership. This is truly about setting your team up for success. And it's fun to make other people happy! Making sure a dinner delivery is on the way before you leave them for the night shift is a good deal for everyone.

3. **Energetically** – On a more intangible but oh-so-important note: Does the energy in the room match what is supposed to be accomplished? This is a trickier question that may take some practicing before you know how to answer it and know what to do about it. If you enter the room with a calm mind, you can feel what the energy is. After all, everything is energy, and people are real energy power plants. If you feel that the energy is off in comparison to the energy that you feel the task warrants, you need to shift the energy in the room. Sometimes you may need to calm the energy levels down to achieve focus, while other times, you may need to infuse more energy, telling

stories or anecdotes with enough charge to shift the energy. Most often, the energy shift that will be required by you is for people to open up. Nothing is as detrimental to a meeting to move forward than locked positions and ego energies. Living in your own non-ego space and daring to be the mature influencer in the room will be an ongoing personal challenge of yours, made much easier from solid mind-training and a meditation practice. With time and practice, your presence alone will shift the energy in the room.

4. **Emotionally** – Is everyone getting heard who should be heard in the room? Are there emotional upsets (both hidden and overt) hindering a good meeting? Are there ego-battles and power-plays going on in the room? With a calm emotional state of your own, you can easily pick up on emotional upsets, without getting sucked into the storm. You are particularly interested in gauging if there are any upsets that will prevent forward-motion for the projects at hand. It is not your responsibility to cheer everyone up, tickle their bellies and stroke their unpredictable egos. What you can do, however, is perform this one trick that works on all people: show them kindness, and facilitate space for them to be heard and seen. Sometimes it's done by telling a joke, but more often it is done by specifically being present with the persons who need it the most and letting the presence guide you to the awareness of what is needed exactly then. When people feel good, they do much better. If someone is way out of line with his or her power trips, you have to take a timeout for a one-on-one. Better to nip that in the bud, as negative emotions not only will spiral to limited thinking in the individual, but it will also poison your whole team.

5. **Inspirationally** – How can you lift people's spirit? Infuse excitement? How can you help ignite a passionate spark? When people are passionate about a project, they give their very best. Lifting their gaze to answer *why* they are undertaking a particular project will add a few cylinders to their force. Sometimes you're in it to win an industry award, and while shallow on a world-peace kind of level, it can be inspiring for many teams. Other times, you are doing your best for a

client who, in turn, is the backbone and primary employer of their small town and, without their business success, would make the town die. Other times you can tap into people's personal passions in the inspiration that you bring. Don't be shy to take some space with this. It means the world for people because it has to do with their contribution in the world. To inspire someone is a reminder or sharing that comes from your authentic self. In spirit. If you are not present with people as you try to inspire them, forget it. It won't work. And keep in mind that inspiration is not the same as motivation. You motivate someone when you have a motive. It's your agenda that you want them to buy. When you inspire someone, on the other hand, you are making room for them to align with their sense of truth and inspiration. This is quite huge—and an awesome assignment for a leader.

> *Try not to become a man of success,*
> *but rather try to become a man of value.*
> —Albert Einstein

As you may have noticed, I have not listed **Intellectual** as one of your contributions. This doesn't mean you should not contribute intellectually, but I know that the point needs no reminder. You will contribute intellectually. We all do that automatically, and we love hearing our own opinions, or what some of us refer to as "facts". By leaving it off the list, I am reminding us all to let the intellectual expert stuff emerge when we have taken care of our other contributions—which, first and foremost, has to do with giving our teams the opportunity to live up to their own greatest potential.

When Phil Jackson, legendary NBA coach and winner of 11 championship rings (!), took on the Chicago Bulls, Michael Jordan was on the team. Everybody made space for this God-like star to shine—and boy were all lights shining on him as he scored and scored. The first thing Coach Jackson allegedly did was to ask this super star to step back, limit his scores, and leave space for the rest of his team. Apparently no record-scorer had ever won a ring and neither had Michael Jordan nor the Chicago Bulls. Coach Jackson worked from the principle that a leader creates space for other people to be as great as they can be—not for themselves to shine the brightest. And that's exactly what Michael Jordan agreed to do; he stepped back, created space for others, and—you guessed it—helped win the Championship ring.

> *My nature elevates their nature.*
> —Phil Jackson, legendary NBA coach

Knowing Your Being

Understanding who you really are may seem like a silly proposition to some of you. It may even seem abstract. What do you mean "Who am I?" — I'm Linda! Look, here I am! I'm a business woman, a mom, a Leo, a consultant, a speaker, a New Yorker, a good friend, a problem solver, a teacher, a meditator—and I'm Swedish!

> *The less well you know yourself,*
> *the more inadequate you feel.*
> —S.I. Mantra

Knowing who you really are has to start by recognizing that you are not your body, nor are you what you do with your body. You are not even your personality, your thoughts, or any labels you—and others—have put on you.

Knowing who you really are can be hard. Not because it's hugely complex but because, in order to get a true answer, we are asking our intellects to step aside. We are asking ourselves to experience ourselves as something more than just a mind-made logical thinker. More so, to experience ourselves as beings with hearts who are deeply wise, as beings who use our bodies as a sophisticated information system, and as beings who, in the deep awareness we find in presence, can connect with everybody else in the world. This makes our intellects uncomfortable. No wonder. Most of us have relied on our intellect for our entire lives and, here we are, treading new grounds. Yikes, says the intellect with a pant. If you find all of this quite fascinating, you're in luck. We'll dig even deeper in to our different intelligences in the SPARK chapter.

Before anything else, you need to know and feel who you are – even underneath your thoughts, traits, values and beliefs; who you are as that presence in you that has occupied many bodies (and opinions); from baby to toddler, child to teenager, and various states of adulthood. It's the same you; it's the same essence. You have had many bodies but have never changed your presence. Isn't that a wild thought? This *you* you are getting to know is not you in relation to your staff, your spouse, your children, your church, or your sports team. Just you as you... you as presence. If you are going to step into *being* a great leader, then knowing who you are from the very core of your being has to serve as your logical first step.

> **I have already lost touch with a couple of people I used to be.**
> —Joan Didion

The only way I can show you who you are is to guide you to stillness, to a spacious place within yourself where your mind-chatter is hushed to silence. You will know who you are by experiencing yourself beyond thought. This really sucks if you're intellect-prone or ego-prone (like most of us are, to various degrees). But believe you me: it can be done and you want to do this. There is no fulfilling leadership success to be had if you don't.

Your nature will never elevate anyone else's nature if you don't feel comfortable with who you are; if you are not in touch with your being. Your own nature. If you don't carry your own weight in the world, to keep you grounded, you'll be flying off to no man's land at the whim of any wind. If you don't feel comfortable in your own skin, it won't matter what you say – people won't look to you as a leader.

So let's start slowly. Can you imagine yourself without your title, without a family role, without a gender, without a name, completely freed from labels? Can you feel yourself there? Who are you there? Can you sense an essence of you beyond all the labels that our minds have made up?

The challenge ahead of you is accepting that knowing yourself deeply has nothing to do with intellectual knowledge, with which we are so familiar. The mind-shift that is necessary to go through is to start experiencing yourself rather than intellectually labeling yourself. That's why we meditate. Even as I write this, I feel my own initial resistance to leaving my familiar me-identifications that my mind holds on to so dearly. And then I can feel my favorite bridging anchor to stillness: my own breathing. My breathing is being done, no thanks to my mind-made self, and there I am, in stillness. That's me.

> *When you are present, when your attention is*
> *fully and intensely in the Now, Being can be felt,*
> *but it can never be understood mentally.*
> —Eckhart Tolle

If the notion of "being beyond the intellect" feels frustrating for you, that's okay. It's just your ego fighting for its survival. Your ego wants everything to be mind-made because that is what it is and what keeps it alive.

When you start experiencing yourself in presence, contributing to this world from simply being, your ego will be threatened. However, you, as your full you, will (perhaps for the first time) feel alive.

I have said it before and I will say it many times: life is only available in the present moment. In other words; as soon as you let yourself be taken out of the present moment, you will stop feeling alive, you will no longer be aware and alert.

> **If the first rule for changing the world is showing up,**
> **who shows up in your case? Who is the you that shows up for**
> **the world? Is it you in presence, alive and alert? Or are you**
> **someone who shows up with grudges, guilt and anger?**
> **Do you show up with worry and fear?**

When the Lehman Brothers collapsed in the fall of 2008, I was on a plane from Stockholm to New York. I caught a glimpse of the headline from the guy in the row in front of me. It felt like a world war type headline, and I quickly got my own paper to find out more about the disaster.

As I read about the largest bankruptcy filing in U.S. history (Lehman Brothers held over $600 billion in assets) and the potential global economic consequences, I wanted the plane to turn around. We were a company with global clients. This was bound to set people in a panic mode with the risk of having budgets pulled from underneath us. My impulse was to get back to the main office and just fix things. Of course, this was an irrational thought, but had I been in Stockholm, I would have wanted to address this catastrophe immediately in front of my staff. I would have wanted to be the big leader, calming everybody down and making things right. Like in a war room, I would have wanted to prepare for the worst and have crisis strategies in place.

Luckily, I didn't ask the pilot to turn around. Not that I have ever heard of a passenger being thrown off a plane mid-air for irrational requests, but what unfolded in my inner business office during my forced absence, with limited ways of communicating back to the office, turned out to be so beneficial for me and my company.

It gave me the time to ask myself how I wanted to show up in a time of crisis. Was I going to show up with guilt, anger, worry and fear? Or was I going to take this opportunity to be the kind of leader who reaps rewards from being calm, constructive and creative, regardless of this world-rattling circumstance?

When I finally returned to Stockholm a week later, I gathered everybody in the conference room. We had already gone through enough mind-training in the office for most of the employees to be comfortable with the lingo. I spoke from the heart and said with conviction that there is a financial crisis going on in the world, but that we have the option of joining the crisis or creating our own reality.

From the bottom of my being, I could feel that we had the choice; that our reality from there on was up to us; that we didn't have to go on the defensive, jump at every negative report and start downsizing to be safe. I shared the strong vision I had for the company in the years to come and how we could make it if we decided to not let the crisis in through our doors. I needed everybody to agree that we wouldn't talk defeat and speak crisis; that we would expect greatness and share the feeling of thriving.

Are you with me? I asked. And everybody agreed. The next few years at the agency were one record-breaking year after another. Not once did we dwell in the stories of all the other agencies that folded around us during this time.

So, who is showing up when you show up? Who is running that inner business of yours anyway? Is it the fears that come with your ego, or is it the calm and clarity that come with your true you? Can you even tell if you are aligned with your true self? (If you can't, don't panic. That's why you're here.)

The greatest leaders are not great, they primarily are.

Knowing if you are coming from fear or truth in any thought you think, in any action you take, and in any situation you face will be your golden ticket to great business success (and a much happier you). When you know what drives you—ego or your true self, fear or truth—you not only get to know yourself better and connect with other people better, it also becomes clear how you can steer yourself in a much more beneficial direction.

Mr. Ego

Hey. You know me. I'm the part in you that's always right. You know how you're always right, right? Well, that's because of me. The more you feed me, the bigger I get.

I'm in everyone, but if you build your life with me as your number one partner, you are sure to be the winner. Not now, but later. We'll have so much fun because we'll beat the shit out of everyone else, and I get to be the hero making *you* the hero: the best, the brightest, the handsomest, and any other superlatives you can think of.

I will make sure that you always strive for more: that you are never satisfied, never happy (happy people are dumb), never feel "good enough" (I hate that expression!), and that you never feel that you are making enough money or that your car is big enough or fast enough or new enough. Deal? And why stop at one car?

With me, you will know from the moment you wake up that you are here to get more, gain more, do more and have more. And then some. When you go to bed, I will remind you that you didn't do enough.

If you call yourself fat or old and start crying, that's me. I'm helpful like that. How would you otherwise better yourself?

If you feel like an idiot, I'm here to tell you that it's true. But stick with me, and I'm sure you'll be really smart one day. First line of business is to make other people think that you're smart. In fact, other people are what this is all about. Other people are the ones we have to crush to be the best.

We have an understanding you and I that we never trust anyone. Okay? Least of all yourself. This gut feeling thing that people talk about? Intuition? Bullshit.

As my favorite saying goes, "If you don't have the tallest building in town (which you must otherwise you are a loser), don't waste your time building yours taller, tear down others' instead." I'm brilliant like that.

It's quite ironic actually because I am really here to help youngsters define an identity for themselves in this time-space continuum in which we live. I'm even here to help people with some survival stuff and make headway here on earth. But that's what's so funny: it never stops there! I keep getting called upon, I keep getting fed (big time!), and my powerful domain keeps growing. It's so awesome. For *me*!

***

Yup, we all have an ego. It's part of being human and serves a great purpose as we make headway here on earth. That's why Mr. Ego is so hard to resist. Much like Mr. Stress, he's here as a survival mechanism, but if you use him for more than his intended purposes, he will, to cut to the chase, destroy you.

Learning to differentiate the ego and the true self within you will be one of the most important steps moving forward with your—true—leadership success. Feel out the EGO vs. TRUE SELF list below for some examples on how to distinguish between the ego and the true self. A warm thank you to my teacher Dr. Robert Holden for deepening my own understanding.

THE EGO

Our ego can also be called our *Learned Self, Mind-made Self* or *Conditioned Self*. You can tell your ego from your true self from numerous clues. **They are all based in fear.**

Your ego will never be happy.
Your ego will never be satisfied.
Your ego...

- wants to create a successful *image* but can't enjoy life
- wants qualifications
- is not ready
- believes success is the salvation *then* you can relax and stop judging yourself
- is *closed* and driven by *fear*
- is an opportunist living separated from everyone and everything
- is a constant source of pain
- will never really feel self-worth
- always feels like something is missing
- is arrogant enough to think that the self-image is real.

The only thing you need to sacrifice for your success is your ego.

TRUE SELF

Our true selves are also called our *Higher Self* or *Authentic Self*. You can distinguish your true self from your ego with a number of characteristics. **They are all based in love.**

Your true self recognizes that you already *are* happiness.
Your true self knows you are worthy.
Your true self...

- is authentic and accepts the "drama" of authenticity
- feels enough being herself
- remembers who she is before showing her face to the world
- is *open* and driven by *love*
- is where your creativity lives
- trusts that life and people are ultimately good
- takes responsibility for everything it experiences
- sees opportunities because it realizes how we are all connected
- knows that separation isn't real.

The only way to get to any valuable success is through complete self-acceptance.

When you look at the EGO vs. TRUE SELF list and start reflecting on what drives you in different situations, you also need to recognize that your actions that come from ego fire up other people's egos.

> *Ego implies unawareness.*
> *Awareness and ego cannot coexist.*
> —Eckhart Tolle

Ego sparks ego because an ego is always in competition. If you walk into a business situation and "remind" everybody who's the boss, you are bound to get competitive reactions. And as much as you want a reaction, I'm willing to bet "I'll show that asshole who's the real boss" wasn't exactly the kind you were looking for.

You still want to be a great leader? Stop competing, stop comparing, stop proving—start serving and step into being.

Understand that you just *being* here holds tremendous power and you have nothing to prove. Whichever side of you—ego or true self—that you feed the most on a consistent basis, is the one that will survive and continue serving you.

One more pointer: when you emphasize a sentence with *me*, you know it's your ego talking. How can you do this to *me*? To *ME*? Note the difference when you emphasize the action rather than the *me*: How can you *do* this to me?

W.I.I.F.M? (What's In It For Me?)

As soon as you show up with any non-forgiveness or fear in their various forms (regret, anger, bitterness, worry, tension, anxiety), you are showing up as an embodiment of your ego. But how is that so bad, you ask? Maybe it's good to be a little guarded and not forgive every bastard who's done me wrong?

The ego is strongly linked to your ability to experience the present moment. Mostly because Mr. Ego really really really doesn't want to you be present. When you are present, he diminishes. He will not survive aliveness, kindness and love. For him, it's better that you are not present. Problem for you is, when you're not, you have effectively cut yourself off as a reliable decision maker.

By inviting your true self to be the one showing up (this is what we will be practicing together), you will become an effective world-changer. Being present saves time because in presence you have access to yourself, to life, and to a very effective knowing.

Don't get me wrong; Mr. Ego is not all bad news. In my experience, the best way to use the ego is as a kick-starter. If you feel disconnected from a deeper sense of why you are here, and therefore can't muster up the excitement to get a project going, you can make use of Mr. Ego.

I brand and design everything I do very well, by my standards. It's important to me. I'm an expert brander and would not want to be caught dead with ugly or useless design. When I give speeches, I want my presentations to look great. When I hold courses, my course material is way beyond what is required. Partly, that is my ego making sure that I am represented in keeping with the perception of me, i.e., my image. (There's another part, too, that drives me, that has to do with the sheer joy of creating beautiful and useful things, and one that loves sharing that, but it's not the whole story). I use this ego-drive to get the best materials produced and then—and here's the real trick—I let go of my ego. The *moment* I start looking for other people's approval of the branding and design of my stuff, I am caught in Mr. Ego and will suffer. No matter if the feedback is bad or full of praise, I will suffer because I am in ego-mode, seeking outside approval. I have effectively given up my own power, I feel incomplete without others' feedback, and I will wonder if I'm good enough.

> **Be independent of the good opinion of other people.**
> —Abraham Maslow

As a leader, you are a huge projection surface for everyone around you. Knowing who you are is a core requirement for making your role a success. If caught in other people's assumptions and projections, you will have an emotional roller-coaster ride that makes puking seem sweet. And I am being serious. It is a true hell-ride to be in a leadership position while allowing yourself to get pummeled by a constant stream of outside forces.

It takes some time to navigate what is really the ego staking its grounds and your truth expressing itself. A good rule of thumb is that ego is closed and tense, whereas true self feels open and relaxed. It is in the relaxed, calm core of yourself that you will find your leadership integrity. Can you feel it?

Please promise me one thing: Never underestimate the sneakiness of Mr. Ego. His livelihood is dependent on getting you to avoid presence, love and kindness. If you find a strategy for feeling great about yourself, he will find ways to make his way back. It will happen every time. The question for you is: how do you respond? Can you stay strong and loving in your truth?

The doors are opened wide for Mr. Ego when you identify yourself with concepts or label yourself and others. Open doors! He'll come waltzing right back in, skillfully blending in with your labeling.

As an example, imagine you've taken a position as the CEO of a company. You define yourself as a great leader. Sounds harmless enough, right? You claim you're a great leader, so you become a great leader. It even works like that New Age affirmation stuff.

Wrong.

The moment you identify yourself as being a great leader, you have effectively invited Mr. Ego to run the show. You see, by doing that, you close yourself off from any other suggestions. Anyone who questions your leadership is wrong. Because you're a great leader. Your mind now has you pegged. In other words, you believe in your own labeling so much so that it has become how you describe yourself. Anything that challenges this is impossible for your ego to process because your ego has created an ideal that can not be questioned. You're a great leader. End of story. Mr. Ego can't afford having that position questioned because it is the be all and end all. When questioned, Mr. Ego can not bend. You know him; he would rather die.

And that's the problem. A leader who can not be questioned is far from being a great leader.

Identification is a mind-made idea of who someone is. Don't make statements of identification or create mind-made absolutes that are closed and rigid, unless you want to be servant to Mr. Ego for the rest of your days. Can you imagine what would happen in your life if you skipped the emotional turmoil of the ego (such as defensiveness, self-righteousness, anger, hurt, betrayal, vengeance, resentment)? Can you imagine the lightness? The mental space? What a leader you could be! You would be a leader who is willing to listen and grow, who would be far more productive and charismatic than any other self-proclaimed Great Leader out there.

Thinking any thought that makes your ego grab a hold of you through identification is like signing up for a neurotic roommate who pays the rent with fake money and refuses to leave.

Integrity and Programming

When I used to introduce myself as a CEO, it was clear from the conversations that followed, that many people immediately assumed a few things about me: that I was tough, needed to be in control, and that I didn't consider other people's feelings. I was also ascribed smartness and big-picture leadership skills—pretty much the usual suspects for a CEO.

Sure, my job included hiring and firing people and saying no to various requests (including promotions and salary levels), and, yes, I could close down an office and in the end be the one who decided who got to work with what. But where along the line did we learn that being the boss discounts being a kind, loving spirit? The programming of greedy senior male executives and bitchy female bosses seem to run deeper than our national deficit.

The irony is that the more people in a non-leading position reinforce the bad-boss idea for leaders, the more new leaders automatically assume that that view is part of the role and play right into it. All this bad-mouthing the boss and negative speculation about company management in the lunchroom undermine harmonious leadership. So why is this still many employees' favorite pastime?

Needless to say, most of our ideas of leaders and business come from our upbringing and programming. But let's not dismiss that as childhood psychology gobbledygook. If these programmed beliefs are left unexamined, they will stick with us, grow worse, and stand in the way for our own potential business greatness. These beliefs, that aren't even ours to begin with, live their own lives within us. You need to check if you actually agree with your own programming about the very job you have or aspire to have.

I know now that I inherited set ideas on what to expect from having a career and "being on the top." Watching my father, who climbed from the bottom to the very top of a global construction company during my first 25 years of life, I was programmed about business and leadership from the beginning. *Life means hard work, there are no shortcuts or free lunches,* and *everything is gained through competition.* His absence spoke louder than anything else, saying, *You have to sacrifice your children's upbringing to have a career.* Oh, plus, *you shouldn't trust anyone.*

My mother was quick to add insult to injury by blaming her career that never happened on the fact that she cared for us children. And that she would be rich if it wasn't for us. Of the few things my parents had in common, being good-looking and never satisfied were definitely two of them. As for being role models for a balanced life between *career and money* versus *happiness and family,* they didn't even come close.

My generation, wedged between the Baby Boomers and Gen X, is quick to ascribe high work ethics as the reason we work all the time. Since I've "been there, done that," on average 70 hours a week, I don't actually think that's the true story.

Speaking for myself, the chasing and proving with relentless hours came from my programming. That's what I had seen and that's what I knew, so that's what I did. I was petrified that having a family would ruin my career and was convinced that any employee who was a hands-on parent would automatically be a bad hire. With hindsight, I have to laugh at how little I knew. You see, time-efficiency and the ability to be present (highly sought-after in business) are two skills that are learned by doing. I am willing to bet that there are no corporate programs in the entire universe that can teach these skills better than the crash-course of being a present parent.

The messages that we get from our parents, verbal or subtle, become guidelines that shape the way we think about pretty much everything in life; amongst them *career versus family* and *making it versus being happy*. I think most of us have similar stories—we just land on different sides of the fence. Whatever understanding you can get of the programming that has shaped you can be immensely valuable in making new choices—just don't let your story put you in a position of blame or deflecting responsibility for your own life. You're all grown up now, so let's become aware and make choices with which we're happy.

In my case, my mom and dad had us kids young and didn't know better. No one had encouraged them, and nothing had evidently prompted them, to find a happy career-family balance. For me, this is all water under the bridge, and I love them dearly.

The gift from our parents with this programming, the golden nugget if you will, is recognizing what our set beliefs about business and leadership have become as a result of these experiences. Only by seeing them and owning them can you make a change and clear your own path. For me, understanding where my programming comes from, actually realizing that I *am* programmed with negative beliefs about business and leadership, work and family life, has been immensely valuable in forming my own happy, healthy and wealthy leadership life, in my own definition of terms.

Over the past decade as a CEO, I have learned that it is possible to reprogram myself. To choose a leadership style that is in line with who I feel I truly am and to choose service offerings that actually help people—while making money! I have also realized the importance of being in love with what I have to offer before offering it to someone else—an insight that applies to actual business offerings and to the inner workings of my own leadership.

This work is truly about you—for you and by you. No other person's opinion or programming should stand in the way of you being you; of you making that beautiful dent in the world you are meant to make. After all, you are the only qualified person for that job.

> *Our own life has to be our message.*
> —Thich Nhat Hanh

Dare to stand for who you are, no matter who you offend by authentically being you. If you can get to truly feeling independent of the good—and bad—opinions of others, you will be free to be yourself. And let's face it: people will always have opinions about what we do, the choices we make and what we look like.

We will never be able to control what other people think. And what they think has at least 99% to do with them (their own programming, their own set beliefs about people, their own emotional needs) and 1% with us. Can you imagine trying to control everyone's opinion about you? I know we all try to some degree, but let's get real—it's useless and plain exhausting! Plus, if you actually really tried, it would make them right about you being controlling, so that would be a little embarrassing.

Dr. Robert Holden, my wonderful Success Coach teacher and a loving thought-leader in positive psychology, often points out that if someone called him orange, he would not be upset. It doesn't resonate at all with him and what he believes about himself. You can call him orange all you want, and he would just laugh. I think you would do the same if someone called you orange. Unless, of course, you are somewhat orange and feel self-conscious about it. By the same token, you can call *any* parent a bad parent, and they will be offended. Why? Because it is impossible to be a parent without having doubts about your parenting abilities. In other words, only if there is a part of you that actually agrees with the judgment of you (orange, bad parent) will you be upset. If you don't agree, it doesn't stick. So what happens in you when people call you controlling? Dishonest? Gay? Sensitive? Egotistical? Pretty? Useless?

**The pain of criticism is not from what the criticizer is saying.
It is from what you already feel about yourself.**

As you decide whether to put weight into something someone is saying about you, use your common sense and your unyielding friend in your inner dialogs (yourself). If one person tells you you're an asshole, you could possibly use this rather poetic judgment for some inner dialog. Does anything ring a bell, or did this come about from a misunderstanding? Is there any merit to what this person is saying? If fifty people look you in the eye and tell you you're an asshole, there most likely is some merit to what they're saying. And you've got some work to do!

If we let go of the idea that we need to control other people or that their opinions have any real bearing on us, we can feel that it's actually okay that people make assumptions and have opinions about us. Go right ahead!

What becomes our job is to make sure that these outside assumptions and opinions don't rock our boat on our mission. Stay in you. Listen. See what your truth is saying. Perhaps you will resonate with some of what is being said. Great, then you will take the hurtful sting as an incitation to examine and better that part of you. Or perhaps you will happily find that the opposite is true of whatever is being said.

Either way, other people's opinions of us can serve as a useful reminder to catch ourselves when we make assumptions about others. Life is just too important to waste on allowing idiots to stop us in our tracks.

"Your time is limited, so don't waste it living someone else's life. Don't be trapped by dogma — which is living with the results of other people's thinking. Don't let the noise of others' opinions drown out your own inner voice. And, most important, have the courage to follow your heart and intuition. They somehow already know what you truly want to become. Everything else is secondary."

—Steve Jobs, commencement address to graduating students at Stanford University on 2005.

Having integrity is one sought-after trait of a great leader. So let's remind ourselves that integrity is not cultivated in our egos. Integrity is setting loving boundaries around you as you honor your true purpose and remember your values. If you feel negative emotions boil up, catch yourself before they take over. Those are guaranteed to come from your ego.

It's still fine to get angry! Just make sure you are quick to observe it as you feel it, know it's not your true core speaking, and remember that it will not do you any good to act on it—especially not in business. Supported by your integrity, your inner knowing knows your truth. It has nothing to prove and rarely has to speak up. Integrity allows life and work to happen through you. Your true qualities will shine through where they are needed.

Again, it's your job to know who you are. When you have connected with that inner presence in you, you will step into that indefinable but palpable power that only a great leader exudes.

Inner Knowing

You know how you just *know* sometimes? How you have thought or said, *That was so strange, but I just knew . . . It didn't make sense, but I just had a feeling!* That is your inner knowing communicating. That is the wiser knowing we access in presence—or what, for some people, may be experienced as flashes of insight.

This inner knowing is what some people call the small voice within, intuition, or the higher self—or even God or The Universe. You can call it Bob for all I care, as long as you recognize that you have an inner guidance system that is connected to other people's guidance systems. That's how you know. In some weird way, we are all connected.

**The worst hire I ever made had that
extremely painful combination of:
a) I made a bad hire and;
b) I knew that I was making a bad hire; but,
c) I went ahead anyway.**

In reflection, I was closed off to my inner knowing as I went through the hiring stages. My mind wasn't open as I convinced myself that I needed a male for the project manager position (otherwise populated only by women), and I had somehow made myself believe that there was a lack of candidates. *There are no good applicants! We have to take what we can get! This is the only guy who seems close enough!*

On paper, he looked good. Not only was he a project manager, he was also a former designer. Perfect for the profile. So with all these on-paper jackpots, I didn't even pull out of my hiring-decision when he decided to wear sunglasses his whole second interview. We were outdoors mind you, but it wasn't sunny, just daytime bright. No one in their right mind would hire someone who is arrogant enough to sit through a whole second interview with sunglasses! I knew this was a bad sign for all the unpleasant stuff that was about to come, but I wasn't in my right mind; I was closed, had made up my mind already, and wanted to get the hiring over with. So I hired him (!). As things went from bad to worse with what turned out to be a womanizing bully (in a country where firing people isn't easy), I would hit myself endlessly for this hiring mistake, mostly upset about the fact that I *knew*. In other words, with a little faith in my inner knowing, and in life, this could have easily been avoided.

Another example, on a happier note, that I have experienced many times in my career is that I have just *known* when we are about to land a new client. Like in the early years with the agency, when we pitched for the largest condom and lust product brand in Scandinavia. Such a fun client to land! And so thought many other talented agencies. It was a hard pitch (pun intended), and I was completely useless for the second round. As with all pitches in those years, it rested on my shoulders to land. I had come down with a terrible flu with limited energy and creativity to muster up anything strategically brilliant. I never use cookie-cutters for pitches but had to resort to some boring, off-the-shelf, non-brilliant stuff that wasn't even unique to them. Disaster. Yet, something felt so right about my meeting with the people from the brand. I had such a strong feeling that we would have plenty to do with each other in the future; a connection, an attraction, a strange certainty... As I walked out of that building I could conclude two things: that was a terrible pitch, and I am sure to walk back in this building many times.

I was so sure that we would get the job (not in my head, there was no logic to this, but in my inner knowing), that I didn't even notice that I had gotten a message from them two days later that said, *call us back, we have some good news.* A decade later, they are still the agency's client, my client and yes, I have been in that building many, many times.

I have yet to talk to professionals about intuitive insight to hear someone who hasn't had a version of the following moments of inner knowing.

I just knew something was off when I hired her, but I didn't listen.

I had a funky feeling about the acquisition, but everything looked fine on paper, so I went ahead. I should have known better.

These statements are expensive deafness to the inner guidance system that is available to anyone willing to hear it. I know I have paid plenty for my refusal to listen.

Your access to your inner knowing will be enhanced by any practice that puts you, as often as possible, in the silence and stillness of the present moment. Why is that? Because it is in silence that you will hear clearly enough to actually listen. Because it is an uncluttered mind that will have space for our connections of inner knowing to happen. These are the connections that make your inner knowing access other people's inner knowing. They belong to the same big awareness and that's how you are connected with everyone and everything else. Language will never be enough for this magic, but I know you know what I'm trying to say. You just know.

What science and I know for sure is that meditation is a useful tool for practicing presence and that mindfulness is a proven way to raise our awareness in the now (the only time there ever is—in business and in life). A calmer mind will help you trust yourself and your inner knowing that is here to help you soar. Or, as my tea bag so poignantly puts it, "To be calm is the highest achievement of the self."

Being in Presence

So, if we can connect with our awesome beings only in the present moment, how do we even know when we are present? And how do we become more present? It seems like being in presence is possible when we sit still with our eyes closed and actually focus on it—but how do we do it in real life?

LIVING IN THE PAST	LIVING IN THE PRESENT MOMENT	LIVING IN THE FUTURE
Regret, guilt, grievances, resentment, anger, sadness, bitterness, and all forms of **non-forgiveness**	Joy, alertness, aliveness, acceptance, knowing, peace, calm, belonging and **love** in any form	Worry, doubt, anxiety, nervousness, stress, tension, uneasiness and **fear** in any form

The above model is a guide for letting your feelings and thoughts reveal to you if you are present or not.

Any feelings or thoughts that have to do with non-forgiveness—such as regret, guilt, grievances, resentment, anger, sadness, or bitterness—are sure to keep your mind in the past. These feelings and thoughts will prevent you from being in the present moment. Likewise, any feelings or thoughts that are based in fear—such as worry, doubt, anxiety, nervousness, stress, tension, or uneasiness—will have your mind leave the present moment as it gets caught up in the fear of the future. The more you choose better feeling thoughts that have to do with love in any shape or form, the more you will be present. These will include joy, alertness, aliveness, acceptance, knowing, peace, calm and belonging.

Thinking that this sounds too soft for business?

Think again.

Without the alertness and clarity available for an uncluttered mind in the present moment, you are left as one of the dull knives in the drawer. *That's* too soft for business. Not being present.

> *There is a raw power that resides in us all,*
> *the kind of force that can alter everything,*
> *forever, in a moment. It is love.*
> —Brendon Burchard

The model contains intellectual pointers for how you can view your emotional states as indicators of your own presence. With time, as you observe yourself in these situations, it will become increasingly easier to choose better feeling thoughts. You will notice that the negative feelings and thoughts you so automatically jumped to before don't actually serve you.

> *I don't do shit 'til I meditate*
> —Russell Simmons, Hip Hop Mogul

As you start living with the intention of bringing your awareness to the present moment and steering yourself to good feeling thoughts, you will also notice how your attitudes and, subsequently, your actions towards other people change. You will skip thoughts of life being unfair and focus on what good this situation has to offer. Great opportunities become visible to you. You will skip being rude to people, even as a reaction to their rudeness, because you now know in your heart of hearts that no one would be rude if they knew how to choose kindness. Great connections become available to you.

Let's relate this to your daily work life. If an employee delivers some sub-par material to you, let's say close to the deadline, you have a couple of choices.

You can either go with the impulse of blame and judgment (which, let's face it, is the easy choice), or, you can choose to be in the accepting reality of presence and quickly find solutions how to help this person make an above-par delivery asap.

With the first route, you will call this person a moron, spending valuable time trying to find answers to the fruitless questions *How the f**k didn't you get what you were supposed to do? Did you even go to school? Do you have any idea how important this is?* Only to round it off with some good old victimhood action *How can you do this to me?? To me?* You ask the idiot to leave your office, and you're the one ending up pulling the all-nighter to meet the deadline. Yeah. Not that smart.

The other route of presence and clarity, which I have to admit is the hard one to choose (especially in that initial minute of making the route choice), is highly recommended. See, there's usually a reason as to why things aren't delivered in the correct way, and sometimes *gasp* it has to do with how you gave the instructions. Other times, there may be a couple of valuable pointers to actually use from this rather unusual way of thinking about the assignment. Other times, the task is simply too complex for a non-senior to undertake. Sure, there are arrogant bastards in the workplace that really should be delivering better material than working on their crowd-funded startup side-project before daring to put this half-assed product on your desk. They might even be out to sabotage you! The risk is slim, but my point is: it doesn't ultimately matter. You have everything to win from *not* jumping on the aggression train, keeping your mind calm and clear, and making your decisions from there.

This is not your regular "avoid having feelings in the workplace" type deal. Emotions will always be a part of our mental systems, whether we suppress them or not. This is you training your mind to choose the kind of thoughts that generate helpful feelings, that make you stay in presence and have access to your full smart self.

People can *feel* if a person is in touch with their inner being. No matter what educational status or achievement merits they come from, they just know. That's what's so fascinating about us humans: we know things without knowing how. And, as soon as you step into your mature self of being, nobody could ask for a better leader.

Mindfulness Attitude: Acceptance

A great business developer accepts things for *where* they are and for *what* they are before they move to change things to what they *want* them to be. It's not that they don't have a strong vision—of course they do—but they have a valuable insight for succeeding: to start where they are.

Many business leaders have a powerful drive to make an impact in the world—to change things for the better. But as long as we fail to accept where we actually currently *are*, it makes it impossible to use the right strategies to get to our vision. Just *seeing* where we are but not *accepting* where we are will not suffice.

You can't see it if you are not prepared to accept it.

There are, of course, many reasons for not seeing or accepting where we are. On a personal level, we all have our reasons for our unaccepting stance—why we turn a blind eye or why we are incessantly judgmental. Perhaps we still choose what is familiar over what is beneficial, even if it's harmful. An unquestioned mind will do that.

Perhaps our egos have run the show for so long that admitting something doesn't work seems far worse than living with the negative consequences of not changing. Perhaps we are simply on autopilot, too exhausted to even notice.

Face reality as it is, not as it was or as you wish it to be.
—Jack Welch

Whatever the reasons, we have to come to see and accept before we can be effective. Whatever it is, let's just face it: I see this is the team I have to work with, and I accept that. I see how much money we've lost, and I accept that. This is my current capacity, and I accept that. I am not wanted here anymore, and I accept that. This is what the competition looks like, and I accept that.

I know you want to jump to the finish line faster than I can say "hold your—"... See, I didn't even have time to say that! Yes, I know results rock, but my point is that you will not get results you're happy with until you start seeing and accepting things first. I'm sorry to have to be the one to break it to you, but this will mean... [pause to take a breath]... don't get mad now... [it's gonna sting]... but you actually have to... [drum-roll]... slow down.

I know, I know. Let's kill the messenger.

Oh wait, that's me! Chances are that stress and bad results will bite you first, so, I'll take my chances.

We can try to give our "refusal to accept the importance of acceptance" a different name, hide our fears, and continue our outlets for our familiar ignorance. But our lack of seeing and accepting will always stand in the way of getting to our vision—our strategies will have the wrong starting point, not to mention how our negative emotions will blur our vision.

> **Do what you have to do. In the meantime, accept what is.**
> —Eckhart Tolle

Time and again, we hear about failed businesses, where management has turned a blind eye for so long that company costs exceed income. What a classic example of not accepting things for where they are and suffering negative consequences! Without real acceptance, your efforts start in the wrong step, removed from reality, and the lack of results leaves you inevitably frustrated (and possibly broke).

The way to start is by creating a little space in your own mind for accepting yourself for where you are, other people for where they are, history for what was, and things for where they are. Then, you can move forward with clarity and flow. That's when real changes can happen. How do we create space in our minds again? For one, by meditating. As you start a meditation practice, you will specifically be training your brain for acceptance. It may or may not happen quickly, but I can promise you one thing: if you don't start, it won't happen.

As you get on your merry acceptance way, you will very likely still have negative emotions come up when you find yourself in an unwanted situation, but now at least you know that it doesn't have to prevent you from seeing clearly because you can meet the situation with an open mind that is prepared to accept what it sees. The acceptance will melt those negative emotions away, and you can move on with a calm, sharp and wise plan for how to reach your vision.

This is why taking a meditation break at work is such a genius idea. With a moment of stillness for your mind, you will get in touch with the acceptance that can make any situation turn around.

Oh the number of times I have been frustrated as I think that the person I'm speaking to is an idiot for not getting it. What I didn't realize for the longest time was that my sheer judgment blocked two imperative areas: One, my own mind-space and, two, my own energetic influence that made the so called idiot even more nervous or defensive or whatever it was that diminished his capacities in the first place.

It's not like people don't notice, at least on some level, when we're loathing them in our minds! So, to be really smart about it, let's skip the judgment, both in thought and in energy. You see, what could be the thing we're afraid of (hence not accepting) is that it is, indeed, our *own* lack of explaining things properly or our *own* under-par hiring capabilities that make us insist that the round peg in front of us should fit into the square hole. Then, the idiocy is on us.

You can go from perceiving people around you as cackling, demanding, and incompetent bastards who all want a piece of you to experiencing them as the real angels they are. Okay, maybe calling them angels is a stretch, but let's at least agree that they are there to help you, if you – let – them. Everything they offer is created for you—it's *your* perception of them, after all! Call it what you will, but if you accept them for what they are, I am sure you will find useful, even angel-like, qualities in everyone.

Drilling a little deeper into our nervous systems, there can be a whole layer cake of conditionings and programming that makes us unaccepting and blind. What I personally love about meditation is that I have not felt a need to intellectually understand all the damages to my own nervous system. Good thing is, I don't have to. Meditation heals the nervous system deeper than a good night's sleep, it gives our brains the chance to rewire, and it helps cultivate an attitude of acceptance that, in turn, will help with the seeing. Again, if you're not afraid to accept what you see, all reasons to fear what you see have vanished. That makes you the sharpest leader in the drawer.

It is, indeed, to our leaders we turn to find the comfort of the insights that follow acceptance. Instead of getting stuck in disbelief about a person's actions or a circumstance, an effective leader does not waste energy on denying what just happened (or speculating about it until the cows come home, you know how that goes).

Accepting people and circumstances for who and what they are saves massive amounts of unnecessarily expended energy —and is key for effective leadership with grand business visions.

So, back to you: The first step in getting to acceptance is to start by accepting who you are. Whatever you see with yourself, accept it. You may not like it, but accept it. You'll see the many workings of your ego and you'll see sides of you that may not be so pretty… You may even be embarrassed about what you see, downright ashamed. So what? Perhaps you've been a dick! At least now, you know!

You also know by now that you have an ego. When you're prepared to accept that you do have an ego, you will not be afraid to see it, and then you can choose to de-crown it and be open to change; you can choose the true you. You are in the driver's seat for any change and you can make it happen right now. But don't tell me I didn't warn you: the real shock may come from your realization of how beautiful you are. What a light you are. How much more wonderful the world is because you are here.

When you suddenly find yourself choosing to be kind instead of pushing to be right, a spacious spot of wisdom opens up in you. When you dare to choose to be curious instead of absolutely needing things to go your way, the joy of having faith is part of your seeing the world. In your choosing of your non-ego based you, you will beam like sunlit gold, inviting people to see you as such. That is the true you. That is the real you, the alive you, the beautiful you.

Now that's quite something to accept.

Mindfulness Attitude: Non-Judging

Much of our mind-chatter—the same stuff that significantly impedes our ability to use our minds effectively—consists of completely useless, repeated judgments. *What an idiot. He can't even speak properly. What a weird checkered shirt. What's with this lumber sexual thing now? And why is it called sexual? Probably because everyone looks gay now a days. Especially where he's from. Wherever that is. He must be Scandinavian. They're all tall. Is Norway still in the EU? No, they never were, or was that Finland? Perhaps that's why he's an idiot. They're all communists. Who tucks a checkered shirt in? Tall, gay communists.*

Left to its own device, our narrative brain takes over. We are programmed to categorize everything we encounter—people, events and things—into good or bad, positive or negative, that our minds have little room for anything else. Talk about waste of time, space and resources!

Our minds are so programmed to comment that they will even chatter as we are watching a beautiful sunset. *Oh, look at that*, the mind says, *What a beautiful sunset. It's orange. And pink. Even more so than yesterday. I think it was more purple yesterday. Or was it the day before?* The commentary of all these labels takes us out of enjoying the experience. There we are, with the opportunity to enjoy a beautiful sunset (life), but we let our minds debate whether it was yesterday or the day before that the sky had a different colored hue. By the same accord, we are so quick to judge, label and categorize anything we encounter in a day that we don't even keep our minds open to opportunities that come our way. We can't think skillfully, so we can't truly experience life.

What if it is not in our better interest to judge anything? What if our acts of constant judging actually stand in the way of assessing situations properly? What if our opinions about everything carry little contribution to the world? It isn't, they do, and they don't.

I can hear the protests going up in many minds. *But it's my job to have opinions! I have to judge things in order to make good decisions! What, am I supposed to just think that everything is okay even though it's not? I am a human label-maker and I'm proud of it!*

For the sake of getting to a more effective use of our minds, let us separate judging (or categorizing) from assessing. This is not meant to split hairs for arguments sake, rather to help weed out helpful assessments from mind-defeating judgments.

Let's start with the basic deal-breaker: Judgmental thoughts clutter your brain unnecessarily. Judgments are fear-based and stressful for your system. They will, with the resulting inevitable dump of stress hormones, activate the more primal parts of your brain, which prevent the use of the executive re-gions of your brain. (Remember, the executive part of the brain that, when accessed, can help you with intellectual greatness, connecting dots, social and emotional intelligence ... the big great stuff). Your executive brain is the big corner office on the top floor and your primal brain is the lobby. When you think judgmental thoughts, it's as if you fill the whole lobby with judgmental little "mini-me"s running around like chickens with their heads cut off as they keep blowing the fuses to the elevators. There's no way to get up to your real office. All these entities are in the way. There's nobody in charge!

Engaging in judgmental thoughts is an automated process that comes from our conditioning and programming with loads of insecurity sprinkled on top. Judging is by far the most favorable of all tools for Mr. Ego. With judgments, he defends his mind-made existence and he can make the judger feel as inad-equate as the judged. How? If I feel insecure about my ability, I can make someone else seem less great to make myself greater. Problem is, that I won't actually feel better from putting someone else down. I will feel worse. And I have helped the other person feel worse, too. Two birds with one stone, and it works every time!

You can lessen your judgmental process by bringing awareness and presence (and, thereby, spaciousness) to it. Making a calm assessment for a business decision in a spacious mind is different from believing every judgmental thought in your head. Can you feel the difference?

Did you ever try to make decisions when you're so stressed out you literally think that you are going to burst? Me too. Didn't work that great. It's the same thing with judgments, but sometimes without the panicky feeling—more so an ongoing cord of tense alertness. Either way, your judgmental you is rendered ineffective.

If you're in a negotiation and your mind goes a hundred miles per hour, keeps commenting and judging every person, word, action and event that is going on before you, you will miss the boat.

You're not listening to the real information. Landing big deals requires far more sophistication than brute force of a judgmental mind. Be it co-workers, bosses, clients, or customers, they can feel your judgments. I even know people in the field of coaching and mindfulness who have judgmental thoughts on what "low level" jerks some professionals are that they want to give courses to. Really? How can you be a passionately engaged and transformative person if you judge the people who you say you want to help? How can you be a great leader if you judge everyone and everything around you?

> *Everybody is a genius. But if you judge a fish by its ability*
> *to climb a tree, it will live its whole life believing that it is stupid.*
> —Albert Einstein

If you can get to a place where thoughts can just "be" without placing such weight on them, you will begin to use your mind more effectively. The thoughts that count, that are actually helpful to you, will have more space to surface.

Here's the new proposition: Bring awareness to your judgments, and choose to not engage in them. Watch them disappear. In the process, you no longer impede your opportunities for good business relationships. Feel yourself become free instead of being stuck.

We all do well by dialing down on believing ourselves to be the best judges for everything. As far as judging goes, we are in the skewed hands of our programming and unquestioned thoughts. Mr. Ego will fight us on this one, but we can remind him of all the times he has proclaimed the situation a disaster only to learn much later that this was the best thing that could ever happen. Perhaps things are more okay than we dare to see them. Perhaps events become better just from us not judging that they are bad.

> *In the moment you forget that you feel bad, do you feel bad?*
> —Byron Katie

The merits of much of the most important insights of your life cannot be scientifically proven. It's up to you to use your inner knowing to see what works best and feels best in your life. When are you the most at peace? What thoughts produce which feelings? Can you choose new thoughts and produce new feelings? How do you feel when you are tangled up in judgment? When you refuse to accept reality for what it is? Are there different outcomes for you between a scenario where you judge, label and categorize, and a scenario where you accept life for what it is? This is your inquiry, your experiments and your life. Take charge of your inner dialogue.

Let the Rubber Hit the Road

So, let's start practicing by seeing where you are. Take a day, or even just an hour, to see how often you label anything in life with a judgment. Be especially aware of how you judge yourself.

Can you walk by a mirror without judging good or bad about yourself? Can you just let yourself *be* there? Practice and take note, without judging your progress, how you judge. Your insight about your own judgment of yourself will carry you over to start noticing your judgmental thoughts about other people, events, and things. The awareness of your own thoughts will, in and of itself, leave room for an increased non-judgmental approach. I can guarantee you that this will clear up a lot of space in your mind to use for better things—for instance, solving a business conundrum or curing one of the world's great problems.

A positive attitude may not solve all your problems,
but it will annoy enough people to make it worth the effort.
—Herm Albright

The Briefing on BEING

I know that not everyone reads a book in the same manner. Some read every word, some skim, some hop from section to section. That's why, at the end of each of the main sections of this book, I'll be giving you a briefing, like this one, so that you can easily go to the brief and catch what you may have missed.

Here is your briefing on Being.

- **Knowing who you are is a prerequisite for being a great leader. Leadership asks; Who are you? Business asks; Why are you here? Your answers can be found in your inner stillness. That's why we meditate!**

- **Actions that come from the idea of doing aren't even close to measuring up to the power of the actions that emanate from being. Actions that arise from your being are consistent with your true desires, your life calling and can draw upon such wonderfulness as your own inner knowing (raise your hand if you've ever "just known something wasn't right," but gone against your feeling by going ahead with the action anyway, to your later dismay).**

- **Life is only available to you in the present moment. The gift of presence is the ability to be calm and sharp, both of which are highly sought-after traits in business, and as a leader. You know that you are present by paying attention to how you are feeling and thinking:**

- Feelings or thoughts of non-forgiveness (such as regret, guilt, grievances, resentment, anger, sadness, or bitterness) are sure to keep your mind in the past.

- Feelings or thoughts that are based in fear (such as worry, doubt, anxiety, nervousness, stress, tension, or uneasiness) will have your mind leave the present moment as it gets caught up in the fear of the future.

- The more you choose better-feeling thoughts that have to do with love in any shape or form, the more you will be present. These will include joy, alertness, aliveness, acceptance, knowing, peace, calm and belonging.

- Most self-development talk or mention of stillness or presence will sound like hogwash to your ego. When you are present and actually start enjoying life in an authentic way, Mr. Ego diminishes. Don't underestimate his sneaky means of getting you back in to competing, comparing and destroying mode. If you don't go there, he's toast. He wants to you back to worrying, stressing, complaining and being pissed off. Don't let him. You can love him at a distance.

- In order to achieve a clear mental state, where real change can happen, you have to be able to tell the difference between Mr. Ego and your true self. Not to mention, to learn how to manage Mr. Stress – he's a tricky one too.

- See your failures and unwanted situations as excellent information for what you don't want – and find your clues in the opposite: what you do want. Every unwanted situation brings this gift to you.

- You can't control other people and you can't control situations – but you can control your reactions to them. This is a pretty powerful notion when you start practicing it!

- When you are less stressed, when you are present, when you know who you are and when you accept where you are, you will be free to be a fearless leader. A sound meditation practice can help you on all those points.

- You primarily attract what you are, not what you say or do. The best way of being a really crappy leader with an unhappy life and constantly questionable results is to believing that you are worthless, undeserving and continuously reminding yourself "Who do you think you are?" with the eerie undertone of "Freaking nobody, that's who!".

- So what's in it for you with this BEING stuff? I'll tell you what's in it for you with knowing who you are and knowing how to be present: You finally have the chance to be a leader for whom people actually want be fully engaged, a leader who has a purposeful vision and who, perhaps for the first time, will really feel alive. You might even realize that you are light and that you are part of a big intriguing world where your actions that come from your true being will have a profound impact on the whole.

So now that you've been briefed, let's move on to some exercises. Ohm.

BEING – Mind-Training Exercise:

As we are embarking on a journey to use our minds in an efficient and beneficial way—with openness, clarity, focus and awareness—we are also learning how to turn more to our own inner knowing for guidance and advice. Ultimately, you know what feels right for you. Knowing what constitutes success for you and putting words on that can help you develop an even stronger inner guidance system.

Here are a few questions about success for you to reflect on and answer. Scribble down what comes to mind.

What is real?

Notes:

What is important?

Notes:

What do I love?

Notes:

What is my joy?

Notes:

Who do I want to be?

Notes:

Needless to say, I don't mean to trick you—but the real deal with this exercise is to reflect on what your thought process was in relation to being, acceptance and judgment as you answered the questions, rather than the questions themselves.

Did you get stuck in thinking that you have no idea what these questions are in relation to? *How can I answer these questions out of thin air? What's the context? What's relevant? What is the right answer?* Perhaps you took them too seriously and got frustrated? Perhaps you have judgments about me, asking the questions? Just observe yourself and the thoughts that have come up.

It's not that the questions aren't interesting for you, if you choose to make them meaningful. What's even more interesting, or should we say informative, are your reactions to them in relation to being.

Perhaps your actual answers to these questions will change over time. For now, make sure to carry these thoughts with you, and use them in your every day life. If you are nowhere near what brings you joy, what you love, and what actually means something to you, you better prepare yourself. Changes are coming. Your answers can steer the way.

BEING – Meditation Practice:

When starting a meditation practice, some people find it helpful to have a teacher who guides them through their meditations. The mind wanders so easily; thoughts come up and attached feelings arise. This mind process can feel like it's in the way for experiencing a meditation in a deep and effective way. Don't be discouraged. There are so many ways to do this, and I am sure you will find one that resonates with you, or perhaps even several that you can switch between.

Throughout this book, we will practice all four different formal types of meditations within Mindfulness Based Stress Reduction. I will also give you pointers from other meditation techniques to help you "get there" without too much frustration. Besides, the more we practice, the longer we can be in a meditative state, without needing constant reminders to come back to the present moment. See how brilliantly that will carry over to the rest of our life?

Breathing Meditation: 5-15 minutes

Simply sit on a chair in a relaxed but alert position. You are in a 90-degree position; your feet flat on the ground, your butt on the chair, your back straight but not strained, your head free from support, your hands resting on your thighs. You can have the back of the chair supporting your back, or not. Close your eyes.

Your simple task with this entire meditation is to follow your breath in and out with your awareness for as long as you have decided. Be aware of the air passing through your nostrils. Feel the air filling up your lungs, making your chest and belly expand. When your mind wanders, bring it back to the awareness of your breathing. Follow the breath out through your air pipes as your chest collapses a bit and the air passes through your nose. Just observe you "being breathed," and don't try to manipulate the breath. Just observe. Perhaps the air is cooler as you breath in. A little warmer as you breathe out. When your mind wanders, bring it back. Just be with you, here. Feel your posture become more alert as you sit in breathing meditation, much as if you had a string attached to the crown of your head, and it is getting pulled up towards the ceiling. Here you are, breathing. Being breathed.

After five, ten, or fifteen minutes, when you are ready to come out of your meditative state, be careful how fast you start moving about. Take your time opening you eyes, feel what the body needs. A few stretches perhaps? A big yawn? To sit and stare for a while? Be sensitive to you. Enjoy feeling relaxed and rejuvenated, as you start moving about with the rest of your day.

Add-On Meditation Trick

Here is one of my favorite methods to get into a meditative state quickly and deeply, or as a stand-alone "quickie."

In this "3-2-1-meditation quickie," we will take three long breaths together, while visualizing different numbers. Sit in a comfortable position. Close your eyes. Start by inhaling and slowly exhale as you visualize the number 3, three times. The visual representations of the three different 3s in your mind should be different from one another, so they really separate. As an example, you can visualize a yellow furry 3, a hand-written 3, and a 3 made out of driftwood. Whatever you choose to see, these are the three different threes on which you focus, completely separate from one another, one at a time, all three during one long exhale. Take another deep inhale and exhale slowly while visualizing the number 2, three times. Same thing here—you visualize three completely different number 2s, separately, and then, one after the other. Take another deep inhale and as you exhale slowly, visualize the number 1, three times.

As you continue with your natural breathing, inhales and exhales, you are entering a deep sense of relaxation. You can add on the mindfulness breathing practice from here, sitting with awareness and the sensation of being breathed for the reminder of the time you have set aside for the meditation. You can also use this meditation trick as a stand-alone "quickie" and be done after your last visualized one. Either way, slowly come "back" to carrying on with life and its tasks. Now, you will have a heightened sense of presence with whatever you turn your attention to.

As with all meditations, I would advise not to use a bell or an alarm to be alerted at the end of the meditation time. There are coaches who recommend that, but I don't. Not that it's a deal-breaker, but having tried both ways (keeping track of my own time and being alerted by an alarm), I have to say that there is something that gets lost when you need something other than your own awareness to wake you up. I have meditated daily since 1996, and it is rare that I don't clock exactly 20 minutes. My body knows; my awareness knows. And if I'm too early, which can happen when my mind is exceptionally racy, I come right back to my meditation after my nano-second peep at my clock.

If you meditate with an alarm, you miss that wonderful opportunity to also train the alertness in your awareness. Having said that, if the alarm is part of what makes it work for you, I say go for it.

Now. On to Focus!

A Crash Course in Miracles

On the morning of May 7, 2015, already dressed in a stunning dress by Bibhu Mohapatra, I sip my tea at the breakfast table, running through the presentation one last time. As a keynote speaker at the Executive Women's Conference in Stockholm, I am only a few hours away from standing in front of three hundred power women, teaching them mind skills and conducting mindfulness meditations.

My preparation with this presentation has been meticulous. Not only am I on a mission of teaching mind skills to leaders in the world, I also recognize the importance of having a professional presentation with compelling evidence, strong graphics and an entertaining flow. (As I mentioned earlier in this book, as a branding expert of many years, my presentations are always perfect and my speaker's notes carefully weighed.)

I am pumped up, ready to give a top-shelf performance that will save these women from burn-out and unhappiness.

I get up from my chair to call a cab. As I do so, I jerk the teacup I am holding, making a splash of tea catapult onto my laptop. *Whoops* I think, *good thing it wasn't that much,* as I wipe the liquid off the keyboard with my napkin. I look at the screen that has turned black. Thinking that it has gone into sleep mode, I brush the touch pad with my fingertips. Nothing. Did it just run out of batteries? I know the answer already, but plug the cord in to keep the panic at bay. I have no backup of the presentation anywhere and am not willing to face the unacceptable consequences should the laptop be dead.

With the cord plugged in, I push the on-button. The familiar tone of an apple computer starting up has never been such sweet music to my ears. I am saved! I can still have the presentation, and my panicked feelings that have seeped into my physical and mental system are slowly subsiding. As soon as the computer is alive again, I focus on the number one priority: to copy my presentation to my Dropbox. I barely have time to think *I can't believe I didn't do that last night!* before the computer goes black again. This time, no matter how many times or ways I push the on-button, it shows no signs of life.

The clock is ticking, and I have to call that cab now. I feel as if I am only semi-attached to my body and the current experience. I see myself leaning towards having severe panic; stepping into that, I would call in sick and focus on blaming myself for blowing this huge opportunity. I feel how it feels to be in that panic and self-blame. I can't think straight, and I can't even find my USB stick where there may be a copy of an earlier version of the presentation. I am pretty sure I had one, but now I can't find it and I'm not sure that I ever did. Did I even bring it to Sweden? I can't find it and, even if I could, another computer would not have the right fonts. This is hopeless.

I conclude that a path of panic is not the right direction for me now. *Choose something else*, I tell myself. *Choose a new thought, one that feels better.* I have never had so many of my own mind-training tools and meditative techniques flash through my mind and my being as I decide that the number one thing to do is to accept that this has happened. I focus all my attention on accepting that I will be on that stage for 20 minutes with no presentation, no video, no visual support that will keep flow and speed. Just me. Sharing what meditation and mind skills have meant for me in my career, my former employees and my current clients. I am trying to go through the presentation in a speak-only format but the order of the slides keeps getting jumbled in my head. I snatch my meditation bells on my way out and put them in my bag with the dead laptop. The elevator is already waiting for me at the top floor and I choose to see it as a good sign.

In the cab ride over, I focus on my breathing, trying to actually *not* think about the order of the presentation. Besides, perhaps the laptop just needs to dry up a little and will work just fine in a while. That makes complete sense in my mind. I put my lipstick on and enter the impressive Bonnier building.

I'm feeling a little dizzy, still struggling with my acceptance. If I knew the computer was gone forever, hopelessly dead, then I would have a better shot at accepting and adapting accordingly. I check in, still hopeful that the dry-ing-up-strategy will work as I make my way straight to the technician's room. I have heard anecdotes from other presenters who claim that some of their best keynote experiences have been the times when they have had technical difficulties and have been forced to wing it. I compare these options. No. Having the presentation wins.

The technician is not rude about it, but basically lets me know in no uncertain terms that I can forget about this laptop. That's the very moment when my real acceptance falls into place.

This is what life is offering me right now...

The first person that pops up in my mind is my dear friend Eva. She has been wanting to go to this event for a long time. Being that it is both cost-prohibitive and that there is a 100-person wait list, it was just not in the cards for her. I call her up and tell her that my computer died, disaster situation, can she please load my font onto her laptop, see if there is an old version of the presentation in my Dropbox, and I'll have someone messenger it over.

Eva says *Sure thing, but why don't we save the money and I'll just take my bike there.* Just then, Jennie, the conference coordinator, walks by to ask how I'm doing with the computer crash problem. I say that my friend Eva will come over and save the day but that I would want her to get a conference ticket for the whole day as a thank you. We get the big thumbs up from Jennie, and Eva joins us during the mid-morning break.

I spend the next program session sitting in the technician's room, rebuilding my presentation, listening to the panel discussion from the stage and feeling such clarity, calm and gratitude. I remember everything I had changed in the presentation from so many iterations ago—all the images, the words, the or-der, the transitions. As I get to filling out the speaker's notes, I stop myself. I have already made friends with the idea that I will do this without a presenta-tion. Now I have it. I don't need the notes. I will speak from the heart and feel the room. When it was my time to speak, that's exactly what I did.

Without notes, my speech became more of a personal connection than an exact performance; it left room for me to express the care that I really feel for other people, rather than trying to "nail it." Being nervous about delivering punches was overshadowed by my deep sense of service. I could feel so clearly what these women needed and longed for. I wanted to make sure that they walked out of there richer than when they walked in, armed with tools to feel better—and having laughed enough to upgrade their bodily chemistry. In that non-scripted moment, I could connect dots I couldn't with scripted notes; tying what the audience had learned from other speakers to the teachings that I am so passionate about sharing. As we all meditated together, I had this awe-inspiring feeling of seeing everyone, even though our eyes were closed. The sound of three hundred women taking their high-heels off to meditate—the air of joy, release, excitement and courage—is a sensation I cherish as an all-time speaking high.

I am not the one to say that I never have given a better speech, but the response from these power women was overwhelming. And this I know for sure: What I learned as I responded to the disaster were real-life examples of what I teach and continue to explore. So what were those learnings?

- For starters, I learned that true acceptance of what has happened, regardless what has actually happened, is key. No labels or blame will help—just acceptance.
- With that, focusing with a clear mind on what the present moment gives me is where I will find answers. There are always solutions, even though they don't look like my own plan.
- Last but not least, in any situation, I keep learning how joyful it is to dare to ask friends for help.

It was as if the so-called disaster that went down was a perfect orchestration to help me get to the next level of reaching people with my life-saving (and business-saving) mind messages. I am in awe of the learnings, which, I have to admit, now also include stop drinking tea by the computer and always make a back-up copy (or two, or three, or fourteen) of my keynote presentations.

Attention is an alchemy that turns
dullness to beauty and anxiety to ease.
—Steve Taylor

Hocus Pocus: Focus

As we turn our attention to Focus, it is fair to share that focusing hasn't always been my strong-suit. I've always been more of a "moving fast between many things" type than a "one thing at a time" type. Once I actually sit down with my tasks, I become more determined to figure things out or to perform well rather than actually loving the stillness in focus. But therein lays the challenge: knowing what to focus on! There is always something pulling me to the next thing, and the next thing, and the next thing.

The subjects (and objects) that are pulling have changed as I have grown older, but the tug is still there. What used to pull me out of focus back then is not the same as now, although climbing trees with the boys on my street actually sounds fun now come to think of it. As I entered the business world I started to share what I believe is the biggest tug for many people: making money. And it's easy to think that the money hunt matters the most, so that's where our focus goes. As irony will have it, however, a total focus on money will not make you feel rich or even be rich. Much of the money pull comes from fear and generates more fear. And what happens to our brains when we feel fear? They don't work that well. It's not quite as simple as just focusing all you've got on money and you'll be rich. Shucks. Besides, we already know that there is so much more than money to a successful and meaningful life! (Don't believe me? Visit a hospital.)

The most important key to experiencing success and meaning
is to know how and what on which to focus.

Focusing on what matters in life sounds easy, doesn't it? Just focus on what matters! Piece of cake. Yet, few people are able to master this skill. As a former girl with ants in her pants, I have a few important things to share on this issue. So, let's see how far we can get, developing your focus, over the following pages.

The Clutter Bomb

The number one reason why we have such trouble focusing is that our heads are a mess of cognitive overload, and so are our hearts. This bombardment of information and demands we all deal with on an ongoing basis constantly pulls us in to a spin-cycle of anger, depression and hopelessness. Email, Twitter, LinkedIn, conference calls, meetings, appointments, social requirements, consumerism, social media, work demands, and family logistics, all tugging your shirt; *I need this by then, I need that now, no give it here first, I can't believe you didn't show up, over here, what happened to you, where's my stuff you promised, have you seen this, have you been there, are you done yet?* The list is too long and too exhausting to mention and leaves us with the apparent question; How in the world can we be expected to focus on things that are meaningful to us when there are so many things competing for our attention?

At no other time in history have humans been so challenged with staying focused. We live in a world of omnipotent distractions.

We could potentially coast through our lives feeling far from good, completely overwhelmed by the distractions flung at us. Here's the huge rub: As we are distracted from that which is actually right in front of us, we are not experiencing life. So there we are, twittering away at our kid's soccer game and answering work emails on the toilet. Swish! What was that? Oh that was your life, Mate. Gone. What do you mean gone? I haven't even started! Well, Mate, that's sort of my point.

So how about you? Are you just going to go with the distracted herd, running your business and doing everything else that's expected of you, all the while reacting to all distractions that come your way? Since life is only available in the present moment, how do you experience life? How do you focus?

Perhaps the world isn't giving you what you want because
based on all your distractions and lack of discipline

it's simply unclear what you are asking for.
—Brendon Burchard

The question of focus sure is a biggie. Luckily, all it takes is some good old ancient wisdom (and a huge scoop of willingness) to help us weather these modern distractions. There are, believe it or not, time-tested ways to train our focus back to things that matter so that we can take command of our own lives.

Whatever we focus on takes increased space in our lives.

Let's repeat that, because it's important.

Whatever we focus on takes increased space in our lives.

This is a metaphysical law and the first intellectual realization we must embrace in order to regain focus. Your outer world is a reflection of your inner world (not vice versa). In other words, you can have as much cool stuff in the physical world as humanly possible, but you can still feel empty on the inside. Outer things don't create your inner reality. If you start on the inside, however, actually understanding that what you put your attention on will create the reality that you perceive, then you have every chance of having the outer world follow suit. Your mental capacity to focus is what largely determines the quality of your life. Your inner stuff creates your outer reality.

As humans, we believe what we think, and we experience feelings that match our thoughts. So our minds start noticing more and more of what they think about and "feel about" and, before we know it, our thoughts turn tangible.

In other words, your mind-spin of thoughts and feelings focuses on something, and that something becomes your mind-spin. This is the exact recipe for having the mind-something materialized. Because the mind wants to support its own reality, the focused thinking is actually showing up in life.

Sounds too weird? Well, sorry, because this is the most fundamental of the metaphysical laws. It rules your life.

That which is like unto itself is drawn.
Metaphysical Law

Now, if it's too weird for you to talk about metaphysics because you can only picture people walking around in aluminum foil hats, we can skip the metaphysical talk and just discuss the relevance of this in our own lives.

On, what we in the school of metaphysics call an acceptably shallow level, you know how it goes already. Because trust me. No matter who you are, you have observed this in life already.

People who genuinely think that there is no good service to be had anywhere always get bad waiters.

People who always complain about how sick and miserable they are, are always sick and miserable.

People who complain about work, rarely have a good day at work.

People who keep repeating that they have no money, never have money.

I remember when I colored my hair pink for the first time (because pink makes me happy, thank you very much). I thought I was so unique. But as it turns out, a lot of women of many different ages color their hair pink! I hadn't seen them before, but now that pink hair was my focus, pink haired people showed up everywhere.

Another shallow example is from back when I traveled by air almost weekly. I would complain over and over about how on this one transatlantic flight I'd been on, I wasn't allowed to eat nuts because of fellow passengers with allergies. And nuts were the only thing I had brought to eat. How crazy was this that I wasn't permitted to eat nuts! And, boy, did I let people hear it.

Lo and behold, 75% of the following flights I was on had people allergic to nuts on them. No nuts for me, and it drove me… crazy!

One day, I stopped talking and complaining about not being able to eat my beloved nuts while flying. Things changed then. Turns out, it's not that common for flights to be nut-free. Only when people like me, attracting such constrictions with incessant whining, fly. When I didn't freak out about nuts, suddenly, there were no nut restrictions on my flights.

I'm sure you have many examples from your own life when you have voiced a condition that turns into your reality. *The printer always jams when I have no time for errors! The checkout line I choose at the supermarket always moves the slowest! It's impossible to find good hires/men/hairdressers nowadays. I never win! So typical! I can't believe it! The train is always late!* We've all experienced the things we focus on growing, in some way. So, let's examine it beyond the silly shallow level. Let's explore this on a business-changing and life-altering level.

If what you think about appears, what would happen if you stop thinking that life is against you?

If what you think about appears, what would happen if you stop thinking that people are idiots?

If what you think about appears, what would happen if you started thinking that people can be trusted?

If what you think about appears, what would happen if you thought of yourself as worthy? Or lovable? Or abundant? Or a gracious contributor to this world?

> ***If all you did was just look for things to appreciate***
> ***you would live a joyous, spectacular life.***
> —Abraham-Hicks

New Focus, New Business

From a business perspective, understanding how we draw things to us is vital. In the early years of placing self-development on my company's agenda, I had pulled my staff together for a day of inspiration. I wanted my staff to understand that what they focused on had a significant impact on how they felt about their workdays and how they could, in turn, impact the business. This was a means to get to terms with both some bullying problems that were going on and my desire to have everyone start taking responsibility for our joint bottom line.

One of the exercises we did was for everyone to list their dream clients on individual pieces of paper, in preparation for a round-table discussion on a new collaborative business plan. A pretty intense discussion followed. It turned out that someone really wanted to work with Swedish Match, a Swedish snuff company with a global portfolio.

Some staff members thought it would be immoral to work with tobacco products, whereas others argued that the company doesn't produce or sell cigarettes and that, as far as snuff goes, it has never been linked to any kind of cancer.

Team No thought that the argument was splitting hairs, since being addicted to nicotine can never be a good thing. Team Yes thought that it wasn't worse than many of the sugar products we already had on our roster of clients. The discussions were intense and people were adamant on both sides. Feelings were stirred and I could see how the Team Yes held the design challenge high. They really wanted to do this. After much discussion, we had to move on.

No more than a couple of days later, the phone rings. At the time, I was sitting with everyone in the open office space and people could easily hear my conversations—especially a member from Team No with his desk facing mine.

The phone call was from Swedish Match. The person on the phone told me that we had been selected to pitch to become their new design agency. I said, "Funny you should call, we have been talking about you at our kick-off. Let me speak to the team and get right back to you."

A couple of employees were already staring at me as I hung up the phone and said, "Listen up everybody, we've been invited to possibly become the agency of record for Swedish Match—should we have another conversation about this?"

My staff wasn't as concerned about the morals of Swedish Match anymore. Instead, they were mesmerized and suspicious: Did we just attract that call to us as a company? Or did I just rig that whole thing?

And, of course, *we* rigged it. By focusing so intensely on it. But I didn't want us to take on the pitch if we weren't open to it, emotionally. I know from experience that we don't win pitches if we have emotional wrinkles on our end. It turned out though, that the staff was all for it now. We pitched, we won, and spent several years working for a company that turned out to be far more aware of how they could contribute to lowering cancer amongst nicotine-addicts than we had thought.

It was exhilarating to witness our own ability to create our own business reality. In addition, we created design we were proud of and had a continuously healthy profit margin. No foil hats involved.

The truism, "That on which you focus, grows" has been a big part of my business life. For years as a CEO, I had a New Business experiment running. Half of my New Business subjects I cold-called and chased. The other half I just focused intently and intensely on, without any particular "doing"—a focus and manifestation exercise of sorts.

After a few years, the experiment yielded pretty consistent results: the focusing half led a little over the chasing half. The big difference was I spent little time and no effort getting the focused clients. I spent an enormous amount of time and effort to land the chased clients.

It also turned out that the clients I had focused into my life were usually better when all levels were accounted for. And no wonder! How they would be as clients, what our collaboration would be like and how we would feel in the process were all part of my focus. When the Renaissance woman in me was satisfied with the scientific testing, I moved to a mixed "focus-chase-focus" New Business approach. I highly recommend it.

You Are Always Right

Let us assume for a while that it is true—what you put a lot of thought and feeling to will show up a lot more in life. What do you focus on? What do you allow to grow in your own mind? If we eavesdropped on your inner voice and mental chatter for a few days, what would we hear?

**Whatever you're thinking, you're always right.
So what do you want to be right about?**

One rainy day, I took the subway from 79th Street. I had debated whether it would be faster to take a cab to my meeting in mid-town, but the subway was right there and the rain was pouring down. There were no cabs in sight and very likely traffic jams ahead. So, I chose the subway.

As I was waiting at the platform, a lady dressed to a tee was pacing beside me. She was fuming, muttering that the subway hadn't come yet, even though she had only been there a few minutes. When I saw the train approaching, I felt compelled to reassure her. *All is well, the train is coming.*

We happened to sit next to each other in the subway car, which gave me the opportunity to study her layers of make-up and large gold earrings. We hadn't been on the train for more than a few seconds when she went on another displeased rant. She couldn't believe we weren't moving yet!

The speakers announced that we were "being held by the dispatcher," and it was unclear when we would be moving. OMG, the woman was right. She voiced her belief that the subway stood still just to mess with her and would move as soon as she got off. And boy did she let everybody know how unhappy she was!

We all learned that she should have taken a cab and that she never takes the subway and that this is a third-world city with a dysfunctional subway system and she always chooses the wrong thing. Always! Life was obviously against her. People around us weren't saying anything to her, but some smiled politely as we all realized that nothing would change this woman's mind about how unfair life was.

I offered a few sound bites of reassurance and even told her that I had a business meeting shortly in mid-town and that I was certain that I will make it. This made the woman more agitated. *How can you be so calm? This is so typical! I can't believe this is happening! And the moment I leave the train to take a cab, the train will move, I just know it.* Time went by and so did her repeated rants.

A man in a suit across from us offered that it would be great if she actually did leave because then the train would finally move. The irony of the statement was lost on her and she stormed out. I can still see her little gold-buckled ballerina shoes on the stairs up to the street as the familiar ding-ding sounded, the doors closed, and we pulled away from the platform.

She got exactly what she focused on, and so did I. The man in the suit chuckled and referred to another law—the law of natural selection. *Hey man, if it takes one sucker to be sacrificed for the whole lot of us to finally move, I'm all for it.*

There are no accidents in the universe.

So, again, what do you currently focus on?

Not focusing on what is meaningful to you means that you are reacting to what's important to others. In other words, what is important to them becomes a ruling force in your life.

Although I believe in the good of people, what's important to most people is not to make you rich. Or successful. Or safe. Or happy. And that's fair enough. Because that's your job.

If you focus on what other people think of you, they will rule your life. If you focus on scarcity and the unfairness of life, you are asking those very things to show up more. If you add feelings of worry and fear about those things, they are sure to be a bigger part of your life.

The only way to be resilient in business—and in life—is to take full responsibility for your own reality. You can choose what you focus on. You can *choose* what you focus on. Ever heard of free will? Well, there it is.

As you start bringing awareness to your choices, you are bound to come up against your programming that, so far, has made you focus on many unhelpful things. It's quite mind-boggling what we have agreed to as ruling forces in our lives.

Remember, your programming comes from the outside, from people and collectives whose primary job is *not* to look after your best interest. Observe what you come up against in your own mind and make up your own present, *calm and alert mind* about what life is to you. What's so great is that you already have everything you need in order to focus on the right things in life because you already *are* everything you need.

Your current state of mind may be chaotic and blurry, but let me assure you—there is nothing wrong with you. Let's just get you into focus.

How To Know What To Focus On

In order for things to be in focus they have to align. If you haven't examined a camera lens for this phenomenon, do. It's fascinating. The mechanics of it reminds me of life and what is true for our beings: In order for you to be in focus, all parts of you need to be aligned.

Your being needs to be aligned with your purpose. You purpose needs to be aligned with your words. Your words need to be aligned with your actions. What you do needs to be aligned with the world. Then the world, in turn, aligns with your being. There, in this alignment, you will find your focus. Here are some pointers to start a dialog with yourself to enter your focused state of being.

1. **Know what excites you.** If you know what tasks and visions excite you, you are in touch with your inspiration. This is not only a powerful place to come from, it is one where you are operating "in spirit." By knowing what excites your true self, you know what to focus on.

2. **Know your umbrella purpose.** Whatever form your life has taken, there are probably at least one or two things you can say with a sentence that starts with "I've always." For example, whether as a high school junior or as a middle manager, perhaps you have always helped people see the best in themselves. That would be a clue to your over-arching purpose or "umbrella" purpose. Perhaps you have always jumped straight to creative solutions and never gotten stuck in the problems. Well, then, *that* is the key to knowing your purpose. Knowing this bigger picture purpose will free you from holding on to the specific forms that life takes because you are free to focus on what really matters.

3. **Know what is important to you.** Even if you have to write down a long list of what is important to you and then go through the pretty daunting task of prioritizing it, top to bottom, do it. When you know what things are important to you, and in what order, you will know what to focus on.

4. **Know that you are here to serve.** When you abandon the idea that business and leadership is about getting away with as much as you possibly can and, instead, recognize that business and leadership is about serving, you will know what to focus on.

5. **Know that you are not a victim.** When you take full responsibility for what comes your way in life, new roads of possibilities will open up for you. Every encounter—it doesn't matter if you call them good or bad—will enrich you. New inspired things will now be available for you to focus on.

6. **Know that whatever you need is available to you.** If you don't have it right now, you don't need it right now, so stop sweating

it—and instead of focusing on lack, you will have the energy to focus on opportunities around you.

7. **Know that multitasking renders you ineffective.** We think that if we do several things at one time, we're beating the impossible time pressure we're under. When you realize that the opposite is true, and that by constantly multitasking you are missing the experience of your own life, you will know what to focus on.

8. **Know your mind.** When you bring disciplined awareness to your mind, you will observe what is driving you, when (and when not) you are present, and if your autopilot has taken over. When you know your mind, you will know what to focus on because you will know *how* to focus.

Exercise: Celebrating You

A helpful way to know what to focus on is to use your imagination. Take a breath and imagine that you are having a company celebration in a few months. Pick a place you like for the venue in your mind. See your family and friends there, along with your colleagues. Someone is holding a speech for you. What would you like them to say? **If you step into the feeling of being completely seen for who you are while contributing to the world, write down how that would be expressed in this speech.**
Notes:

Summed up in just a couple of keywords:
Notes:

When you reflect on the eight points of focus above and know how to answer them in a way that resonates with your being, you will know what to focus on. The speech scenario helps make it real in your mind. Your old programming will still challenge you, but now you can walk taller with a natural sense of knowing what you want. This is a fantastic step—a leap, in fact.

Which leads us to the other big thing we acutely need to become aware of on our quest to excellent focus: our autopilot. Few things stand in our way of focusing on what matters as the negative impact of our autopilots.

Mr. Autopilot

So, you think we haven't met before? Well. Isn't that a fine how-do-you-do?

I might not be as sexy as Mr. Stress or as macho as Mr. Ego, but you'd be in a fine mess without me. Why do those two get all the headlines, anyway?

I'd like to see what would happen if I disappeared from your life.

Without me, you'd have no life! It's me you have to thank for that amazing ability you have to breathe automatically. Imagine if you had to think about what to do with your lungs!

Walking without having to relearn how, every single time? Yes. You can thank me for that, too.

Ever reached for a glass before it fell to the ground? You're welcome.

When you go to the office, do you have to think through every single step of how to get there? *Turn the car engine off. Open the car door. Put the left leg on the ground first. Shut the car door. Wait for the right time to enter the revolving doors to the building. Walk across the lobby. Push the elevator button. Say good morning to someone. Find the office. Sit down on the chair...*

Didn't think so.

The reason you can do all of those things without thinking, every time you go to work, is because I'm there on the job for you.

You could never multitask without me.

As far as I'm concerned, I'm a much harder worker than stress and ego put together.

You call on me *all the time*. Even now you might be mindlessly snacking while you're reading. You even rely on me for scenarios where you really should be fully conscious. Like when you're driving a car. With me behind the wheel of your brain, you think it's fine to pick up that cell phone. Not cool of course. But don't blame me.

I'm so busy helping you supervise your children's homework, do the dishes and plan next quarter's budget—at the same time— that I don't have time for your complaints. Why would it be my problem that, the more you let me take over, the more you're missing your life?

I need a vacation from you, but I'm never going to get one. Ever. So don't ask me for any favors. My job is to take over as much work as possible from you. Forever. What's yours?

***

Our lives can be viewed as a constant battle between the Autopilot and the Alive You. Question: Will the programmed, mechanical you take over, or will an awake, alive and vibrant you be the victor? If you're like most of us, you let your mind wander and the autopilot take over more than half of your awakened time. You're missing out on your life all this time! Somebody call somebody!

As superheroesque as Mr. Stress is for his fight-flight-freeze skills (sounds too cool for school), Mr. Autopilot is quite impressive, too. And he's busy! He makes sure we walk and breathe and get on and off the bus without tripping. He helps us catch our baby as it falls from our lap just as we're eating a spoonful of chicken soup. Mr. Autopilot even saves lives! Imagine if a paramedic had to stop and think about how to do CPR. Or if a surgeon had to refer to his notes in order to save a patient from a stroke.

Mr. Autopilot is important indeed. This is the good Mr. Autopilot.

Much to our benefit, it seems, Mr. Autopilot steps in and takes over as soon as we need more things done at one time. I can walk, lock the door, speak on the phone, balance my teacup, put on lipstick and wave to the neighbor to wait with the elevator in one go. Thanks Mr. Autopilot! Who doesn't need help to be a multitasking master sometimes to get a move on in this world? (But wait! Did I put on mismatching shoes? Because that can happen when Mr. Autopilot is on overdrive.)

Mr. Autopilot also helps our brains sort lots of similar data into bigger general piles so that we can more easily categorize things in our thinking. We don't have to think about every single movement we make. The way that we never forget how to ride a bike after we learn is just one of a million examples of his workings. This is quite nifty for making our lives easier—and even possible, really.

But Mr. Autopilot has a dark side. A big but. Our brains, unfortunately, don't know when to stop engaging him. As a result, we are left with not only the Mr. Good Autopilot, but also with the big-butted Mr. Bad Autopilot. As with the rest of the crew, we don't know when to stop calling him in to do his job. We quickly go from automatically hopping on the escalator at work to letting Mr. Autopilot take over tasks that are unsuitable or even dangerous for doing in an unaware (automated) state.

Take, as an example, the human mechanics of driving a car. Much of it is with the help of Mr. Autopilot. However (big but), results are devastating when too much of our conscious awareness is checked out in the comfort of the autopilot. This is why many accidents happen.

Even in relationships we have far too many surprising accidents than we thought we bargained for. All the automatic phrases, vacant responses, and taking each other for granted have ruined many relationships. Or, as another example, we do the dishes and take the opportunity to go through tomorrow's presentation in our heads. Seems harmless. But there's a risk that the dishes only get half-washed or, even worse, a dangerous scenario that a glass breaks and, as you are not connected with your senses in your mind-wandering state, you cut your hand. Sounds implausible perhaps. But one thing is guaranteed: You keep programming yourself to miss out on life.

Christopher Reeves, the one and only Superman in my book, was paralyzed from a horseback riding accident in 2000. The world was shocked at this seemingly cruel cosmic joke. I can still hear famous funny guy Chris Rock echo in disbelief "Superman can't walk. Superman can't walk." We couldn't believe it. It was just too absurd.

Mr. Reeves, though, had a different view. In interviews that followed, he said two things in particular that had a profound impact on me.

One is that he didn't really become superman until after the accident.

The other is directly related to the subject of focus and liability. He described himself as always being very present when he was on a horseback. He loved the synchronicity between himself and the horse, one that could only be found in the present moment. The moment the accident happened, he described how his mind suddenly was elsewhere. He was not present. He was not in sync. That's when he fell so badly that he was paralyzed for life. Superman couldn't walk.

When we let our minds wander, Mr. Autopilot takes over.
And rest assured, he is ill equipped and completely useless
for many of the tasks that life will ask you to master.

Who Stole My Cookie?

With Mr. Autopilot at the helm, we also do things we later don't remember having done. How many snacks have you eaten in front of your computer and been sincerely surprised when they are suddenly gone? Hey, who ate my sandwich? Give me back my cookie! What happened to my chocolate bar? Hey, where did my life go?

With Mr. Autopilot, we keep doing things without reflecting on whether they are good choices for us—or for others! We seem fine with our internal answer: *because I've always done it this way.* How many relationships do you still have that aren't serving you because of the sheer comfort of the familiar? How much is your company's role in the world impeded from being on autopilot, doing "business as usual"? How many people do you think stick with their jobs, even though they hate their work environment? Who's doing who a favor with that? No one to nobody.

If the bad autopilot stopped at forgetting where we put our keys, we could get one of those beepy key finders and that would be that. But you know how it goes; it doesn't stop there.

Our lives are so pressured to the minute that we often forget things we neither want to nor should forget. We do things with no consideration of consequences, as we do them without awareness. And we're paying a high price for letting our lives be ruled by a bad autopilot.

The worst: We are literally missing out on life.
The middle worst: We make unnecessary mistakes.
The kind of bad: We call our new client by the wrong name.
The kind of bad but cute: We go the wrong way on the subway.

What all of these have in common: You are not being present. Mr. Autopilot is running the whole show.

Uptown Oopsie

My fellow school parent Justin is quite a terrific example of how the autopilot can be, simply, unhelpful. Every morning, Justin and I would meet during the morning drop-off at school. Every morning, he would greet me with "Good morning, Linda," and every morning, I would reply, "Good morning, Justin, how are you doing?"

We had done this for a little over a year when, one night, we met for a parent meeting at school. Justin and I had already met that morning, yet when he saw me again that evening, he said, "Good morning, Linda." I chuckled and said, "Well, good *evening*, Justin, how are you doing?" Justin heard his autopilot error and laughed it off.

The next morning, we met again and he said, "Good morning, Linda. I have to tell you something." It turned out, that not only had he used the autopilot as he greeted me with a good morning in the evening, but when the meeting was over, he had taken the subway downtown—the same way he goes to work every morning. Problem is, he lives uptown.

I think we can all relate to Justin. Taking the subway the wrong way, misplacing things, pouring orange juice in our cereal, or calling our partner our ex-partner's name (whoops!). Some of us don't even remember one day from another, and most of us have walked into a room many times without remembering why we're there in the first place. Most examples are cute little things we can laugh off. But when we start realizing the bigger impact of the bad autopilot on our lives, we have identified a huge liability.

One of the worst (yet most common) outcomes of letting Mr. Bad Autopilot operate within your inner business would be the resistance to try something new. The autopilot lets your business keep chugging along even though you haven't updated your marketing plan since Facebook became a verb.

Can you think of any potential unwanted business effects you are experiencing from your autopilot? Can you detect your own level of awareness in the meeting with your coworkers, your clients, your tasks, or your investments? Is there something you could be missing, as you are not being alert in your actions? When you pitch for a new client? When you present for the board? When you hire someone? (Ooooh, that's a snoozing biggie). I bet when examined, quite a few dangers lurk with most situations—and opportunities arise.

Autopilot Unplugged

If you want to bring an aware light to the workings of Mr. Autopilot and lessen the negative effects, meditation is an effective antidote. Through meditation, we learn to deflect our natural inclination to simplify things that need our aware attention. Step by step, you regain control of situations that you currently leave up to chance, programming, and, even worse, other people.

The reason meditation works is the same reason practice makes perfect with just about anything—we train our minds to be fully aware in the areas where our bodies and minds are the most automatic, namely breathing and moving. With that, we grow increasingly aware of our autopilot in real life.

When we train to become aware of our body movements in its simplest forms—sitting, standing, and walking—being aware of any movements become our new automated function and being aware of other people's states of mind and intention becomes possible.

**Through meditation, we train our brains
to know what we are doing—and where we are going.
See how useful this is in business?**

When I started my career, I was not a good negotiator. I had a hard time talking about money and would rather avoid the subject altogether. (Programed negatively about money, anyone?). As a consequence, I often had run-ins with people about money. Either the client was annoyed; *Why hadn't I flagged for the extra costs? Why do you send an invoice this late?* or I was annoyed; *Why do I have to work and not get paid what the job I'm doing is worth?* I didn't get why people were so difficult to talk to about money!

As I gained some space in myself (the "gap" that we talk about in meditation), I could see that the only common denominator between these money problem people was, ehm, me! (Ouch!) As much as it hurt my ego, though, it was time to fess up to the idea that the money issues I kept running into had to do with my own thinking. I could suddenly feel how the unwanted money results stemmed from the discomfort and fear I felt around money. I mean, how could they not? Up until that point, I simply hadn't realized that I made all these choices on autopilot—that a programmed part of myself had taken over. I hadn't seen my own contributing role as the scenes were happening; it was just the way it was, and I chopped it up to other people's fault.

That's how it goes when we are unaware of our personal responsibility of how we experience life—when we cover our discomfort and fear by letting Mr. Autopilot run the show.

Years after I had woken up from my money-related autopilot, I took the train down to Gothenburg to negotiate a contract with a new potential client. Although I had already learned to keep my aware focus top of mind and had practiced many times to bypass my programming, it still felt like a big challenge ahead. This time, I was negotiating on a new, global level that could put the agency on the top shelf of international accounts. As I approached the negotiation, I was acutely aware that when the stakes are high, we all easily fall back to our old fears.

As a means of being aware in my focus, I kept connecting with a feeling in my heart that was so convinced that we could contribute greatly to this global consumer goods giant. I kept feeling my breath and my movements as I entered the room. Presence was my best weapon. And that's when I realized: The only way to win this was to let it go.

I was surprised at my own conclusion, but it felt right. We all know how to smell fear and desperation, and this time, albeit on a more subtle level, I didn't want to lose this opportunity to my own lack of mind. I really didn't want to blow it for my staff and the company, so blowing it was exactly what I had to be prepared to do. It was an intense inner moment for me leading up to the table. As I started talking to the Head of Purchasing, I realized that this would be far from a walk in the park.

There I was, selling creative services to someone whose days are spent negotiating paper mass prices. She had a fixed idea of what she would pay per hour for creative work, and talking about anything other than hourly fees was out of the question. Too bad for me, as much of what I was selling were programs, workshops and actual results. Per hour consulting is a slippery slope that has left many agencies broke. As she continued her dis-attached, For My Information-style presentation, I reached a fork in the road. Play along and say yes to something that I actually don't believe in as a model for my company or make my point come across with vigor, with the risk of losing the whole deal?

Mr. Autopilot didn't want me to rock the boat. He wanted me to secure the deal and then later let me bitch about what cheap bastards these money-problem people are. In that scenario, I would undersell us per hour and be forced to do what many agencies do—add on hours to make ends meet. Safe and slightly dishonest. Business as usual. By now though, the answer was in the question. I chose the latter.

I asked the Head of Purchasing how long it takes to come up with a name for a new brand. I argued that if we are basing our whole contract on a per-hourly basis, there must be a solid reason to do so. If she didn't know how long creative work took, then what was the point? But she couldn't answer. "Okay," I said, "perhaps it's hard with a new brand name—it's such a huge undertaking—so how about new product names? How long would that take?" She couldn't answer this one either and was now visibly annoyed.

I wanted us to find a common understanding that selling creative services by the hour alone was not a great idea and that we could spend some time discussing solutions. In my thorough recommendation for them, I had already outlined our trend forecast methods, cutting edge emotional consumer workshops, and unique concept development tools over diverse markets. These were not hourly undertakings, but rather products to purchase that had taken us years to develop with specific results for them. But she wouldn't have it.

To my big surprise, I stood up and said that it had been a pleasure meeting them and that I would take an earlier train back to Stockholm. If someone could point me to where I would get a hold of a taxi service, that would be great. On the inside, I was shocked at my actions. It seemed so rude! But it also felt right. I had a whole staff to defend and a company to lead, and I could feel the strength from valuing us so highly that I was willing to walk away from a half-assed deal, albeit a global one. This is when the Global Brand Director jumped in and said "Linda, go to the cafeteria on the ground floor, and I'll meet you there in a while. The rest of us stay here." I felt like a kindergarten kid that had been separated from a fistfight and now needed to wait for the disappointing feedback. Another programmed memory. And no one was really meeting my cheery goodbyes as I exited the room.

After what felt like a very long cup of tea, the Global Brand guy showed up at the table. "We're good to go", he said. "Your recommendation has been approved. As for production, you agree to the hourly terms." My inner business had a sudden company party. "Thank you. I can't wait to start working with you," I said, not even realizing that this global account would be one of the most fun accounts of my branding career.

The successful man is the average man, focused.
—Ralph Waldo Emerson

In order to reach a new level in business and leadership, we need to learn how to get out of our reactive states and programmed behavior as often as possible. If we create a mental space in ourselves to question our pre-programmed attitudes, we can gain control of our own lives. We think we're so safe and sane by doing what we've always done, even though we're not happy with the results.

No one will take care of your inner business but you because no one *can* take care of your inner business but you. This really should be earth-shattering information for anyone. You will never live up to your potential and purpose or even feel that you are really alive unless you start taking some real responsibility for how you lead your life.

Becoming aware of whether the autopilot's actions are benefiting you or hindering you is one step in the right direction of making your life happen for you.

Another useful step is to take a good look at your attitude towards life. And by that I mean—how do you really believe life is happening?

Attitude Levels

Your outlook on life and your attitude about how life happens determines whether you will ever live up to your true potential as a great leader. There are two outlook levels we will discuss here:

Life happens *to* me.
Life happens *for* me.

- Reactive
- Looking to blame
- Victimhood
- Life is unfair
- Ego-driven
- Contracted awareness

- Proactive
- Takes responsibility
- Creates opportunities
- Life is ultimately good
- Driven by true self
- Expanded awareness

Nothing in life is static, and neither are these levels. You are not parked on the one level, nor do you graduate to another level when insight strikes. In any given day, you can have moments from both of these levels. The question is, how much of the time can you minimize being on the first level?

1. Life Happens To Me

The most basic, unaware and unquestioned outlook on how life happens is to believe that life happens *to* me. With this level of awareness, you are an unassuming receiver of whatever life throws your way, with no creative powers. Victimhood and cynicism rule your worldview and pointing blame is a much-used knee-jerk reaction.

Believe you me, you don't want to catch yourself for too long on level one. This is Mr. Ego's headquarters that offers virtually no authentic inner satisfaction.

Here, you believe that life is unfair, so you don't even have to take responsibility that you are just "doing what it takes" to get ahead, even if it means blaming the competition or your mother for your own immoral choices.

This is the level where blaming others for anything that goes wrong in your life is automatic, even your own decisions.

"I didn't have a choice," "It's not my fault," and "It wasn't me" are commonly uttered sound-bites on this level.

You don't trust anyone. Your reaction is to try to control everything and everyone, usually by putting your nose where it shouldn't be, flexing your boss/parent/disgruntled citizen card to make it happen. If it doesn't work, which is most of the time, you will punish everybody by being in a foul mood.

This level offers no creativity, no happiness, and no innovative skills. How could it? Proving that everything is everyone else's fault consumes a whole lot of energy and closes up your mind. You completely miss the opportunity to see anything that happens in your life as an invitation to grow, learn and flourish.

On a "life happens to me" level of consciousness, it is impossible to be a great leader.

Few people are likely to voluntarily admit that they operate with this kind of attitude. But life is rarely black and white, and the same attitude produces many "milder" versions of what I just described.

For instance, on this level, a lost client pitch is a disaster. It seems fair to think of losing as something devastating—something that we are entitled to be really disappointed about (and let everybody know it and feel it). We can even start pointing fingers of blame. How will we otherwise know who to fire for the next pitch?

But that's the point. A lost pitch can be a blessing. I have countless examples where I, with the benefit of hindsight, can thank higher forces for not having landed a client I so desperately believed I wanted.

Thinking of setbacks as disasters depletes you of energy. This level is exhausting! Resilience is gained by being open and flexible to not knowing everything and accepting things *regardless of circumstance*. Perhaps what you think of as the best solution is the true disaster? How can you be so sure? But openness is not part of this level, and you will continue to see losing as devastating. People around you will continue to be weary that the fingers will be pointed at them. Inevitably, they will. When you feel pain, you find someone to blame.

Let's take it back to a simple example. You stub your toe. Man, that hurts. Looks like nothing from the outside, but makes a grown man wanna cry. If you stub your toe and think that life happens *to* you, you will feel the pain, concentrate on the f-ing pain; you will probably kick the chair again since you had pegged the chair as the villain in the drama. If there's a person to blame you will go for it: *Who put this chair here? I said who – put – this – chair – here?!? An idiot, that's who!* You feel more pain from kicking the chair again. Problem is, any pent-up anger that may have been the reason that you stubbed the toe or wanted to scream at someone in the first place will still be in your body—because you can't stub or blame your way into releasing real anger. Hopping around on one leg won't heal the depths of your fears either. Being pissed and angry will, guaranteed, make your day feel worse, as well as the day of those around you. Lose-lose, poor you, and who are you gonna yell at now?

As unacceptable as this attitude sounds, the strange thing is that "life happens *to* me" seems to be the most common of life attitudes. This is, unbelievably, where most people spend most of their days!

If you've never questioned yourself on this level, this is a hard one to see. Most of us have learned how to dress up the most obvious traits of this low-level consciousness into something that looks a little prettier than a monster bully. If we try really hard, most of us can find circumstances or world events to explain why we're stuck in our misfortune. In reality, this means that what we experience as something bad in our lives is something we feel victimized by because it was not our fault.

Don't get me wrong. Of course tragic accidents can happen, and you can't personally take responsibility for every single thing that happens in the universe.

And I hear:

You're damn straight, I can't prevent the stock market from crashing, can I? And now look at me! Destitute!

or

Of course it wasn't my fault that my husband died. That would be so cruel to say! And now I have nothing!

or

I never stood a chance, growing up in poverty without a proper education. How dare you say that I can't complain about my sorry lot in life?

Whatever is true for you is true for you, and I am not on a quest of taking that away from you. What I'm offering is an outlook where you absolutely can take responsibility for how you react to these events, which, in turn, will be directed by the attitude you hold as to how you believe life happens.

> **If I had a god, which I don't, it would be reality. Because it rules.**
> —Byron Katie

If you really believe that you are the innocent recipient of the events from "out there" (in other words, that you are separate from life and everything that's going on), you will always be afraid, and you will never feel powerful. You are a part of all life. I know how hard this is to recognize or even agree to be true. You don't have to agree. You are still part of life. You are part of making all this happen. Everyone is part of making everything happen, and what you can decide is your attitude about it. My hot tip: Be mindful of what you are choosing.

> **With a "life happens to me" attitude,**
> **you don't realize that life just is what it is,**
> **no offense to you.**

We don't know what the full scope of life is. We don't even know what the creative consciousness is. We know something is there, growing the flowers and our hair, while making it possible to have intuition about that which seems to be separate from us. But you can feel it, so you must be connected to it somehow.

We don't know what it is but we know we are part of it. Your ego will not agree with this, not even the notion that life is ultimately good.

This is a big picture concept, that there is something *ultimately* good about life. At least, life just is, and it's not against you.

If you don't believe that there is enough goodness in the world to go around, this will be a hard life for you. Please bear with me because believing in a greater good might actually be logical.

I have friends who have been forcefully pushed off the corporate ladder; who have lost their spouses and all their children; who have lost everything they owned; who are terminally ill, unemployed and physically handicapped. I have rich friends, beautiful friends, influential and famous friends, friends with powerful positions, and friends that truly have it all. But you would be surprised who among all these friends are the happiest and the most functional.

The ones who make great leaders are not the ones who think they are victims of circumstance and can thank their shiny careers to their own hard work. It is the ones who can see a bigger connection between people, events, and life situations who ultimately thrive.

According to mystic expert Caroline Myss, we were all born with the Victim as one of our four given archetypes. She also says that the Victim archetype is here to teach us how to turn Victimhood into Victory. Well, if it's true, that we all have a Victim inside us, then let's view it as an opportunity to learn how to become victorious and get over this "poor me" attitude already. There's nothing poor about you! There's nothing wrong with you! You're here, right? Good, so let's get to the next level.

2. Life Happens _For_ Me

We have all heard the saying, "If life brings you lemons, make lemonade." It's cute, and I, for one, start thinking about kids and darling little lemonade stands with hand-written signs. Sweet as it is, the metaphor is really encouraging us to do more than just seize the moment with some cheery optimism. It points to a pretty deep insight—that you can choose to look at life as happening _for_ you instead of _to_ you. "A sour situation? Let's skip the judgment, and we're left with a situation. Already it's more palatable. Not what I had planned, mind you, but let's see what possibilities I am missing."

With that, some radical responsibility needs adding to the refreshing mix.

If life is happening _for_ you, everything you encounter and experience can be viewed as a gift. Not minus the sour stuff or the bad stuff. Everything. From that gift for you, an actual learning experience could be had, followed by healing and growth.

On this level, you take responsibility for your actions, including those that happen _to_ you. If faced with hardship or assholes, you don't go into a frenzy of finger pointing and blame. You choose right there to accept the situation, do something about the situation or to leave the situation. That's it.

Since you trust yourself, you see no reason to be suspicious of people for the sake of suspicion. Your mind is calm and alert, and you trust your own guidance system to tell you when things should be given your scrutinizing eagle eye.

Your opportunity, on this level of awareness and shift in attitude, is that you will see the possibilities because you don't dismiss the situation as wrong, fruitless, useless and unacceptable—and my guess is that the impact of the shift will be major.

If a door closes, you don't waste your time and energy sulking about not getting your way. You are already focused on seeing new opportunities. And, as you look for a new door, you may even have an insight as to why the other door closed. Patience brings those kinds of gifts.

The reason you want every single thing that you want, is because you think you will feel really good when you get there. But, if you don't feel really good on your way to there, you can't get there. You have to be satisfied with what-is while you're reaching for more.
—Abraham-Hicks

Have you noticed that when you're angry, you're more likely to attract more negative things? As if it wasn't enough that you're angry because you stubbed your toe; now, you just missed your train and your phone ran out of battery power. It seems that whatever we are, as beings or organisms, that we want to prove ourselves right.

It goes something like this: "Life hurts — let me prove it — toe-stubbing — pain — see!?!".

Although it is not yet proven, I am sure that the scientific community eventually will conclude that, sometimes in life, shit actually just happens, for no particular reason. But to think that things happen in isolation is just plain futile.

With your "life is *for* you" attitude, you still feel the pain of the toe (actual and metaphorical), but at least you are open to the messages that other parts of you are trying to send. You check yourself. Perhaps you discover that you had pent-up anger that made you stop in sudden pain. Perhaps you're fine, both on the inside and the outside, toe included, no harm done. At least your brain will not be shut off from the primal workings of the amygdala. Instead, you'll have access to your executive brain and snatch your battery charger as you leave the house. With an open attitude, you will win every time.

> *A change of circumstance happens as a result of*
> *a change in your consciousness.*
> —Neville Goddard

When you live with an expanded awareness, you start looking for meaning and opportunities from what happens in life. You are effectively jumping up to a new leadership level and taking responsibility for your life. Having faith that life is ultimately good may not make absolute sense, but for anyone willing to try, great rewards are waiting to be enjoyed.

Mindfulness Attitude: Patience

Throughout the history of philosophy and psychology, patience has indeed been coined a virtue. *Good things come to those who wait.* In mindfulness and in the world of meditation, patience helps us bring our awareness to the present moment. With patience, we are not adding a stressful feeling of getting out of the now. We are where we are, awake to the possibilities that arise at the only moment they actually can arise—in the present moment.

> *"You can't make money in the future. You can't make*
> *money in the past. You have to be present"*
> —Russell Simmons, Hip Hop Mogul

Impatience prevents us from being present, and that's when we start to make mistakes. We seem challenged with patience in different areas in our lives. What you find a breeze to be patient about will frustrate me to tears, and vice versa. Patience in certain areas has been quite easy for me—but definitely not in the workplace. It has always annoyed the hell out of me when people don't understand what, to me, is a simple concept. Let's get on the tasks already! But oh no, they don't even understand step one.

Are they idiots? Watch me explain it for the third time and a curtain is pulled over my eyes. I can't stand slow thinkers! Until I can. Until I remind myself that everything has its time. That I have a choice to explain it again in a completely different way. That I can find a better way. That this topic might be too complex for this person to understand. That what I am saying makes no sense or is of little value. At least right now. Now is obviously not the time. How do I know? Because it's not happening.

What may bring us all together under one big impatience umbrella is our unwillingness to be patient with ourselves. No other person is a harsher critic to us than ourselves. Until we realize that it really should be the opposite. If we have one constant person in our lives, it is us, ourselves. You for yourself, and me for myself. Any other strategy than making us patient and encouraging towards ourselves is a crap strategy.

No one ever flourished from harshness. (In Mr. Ego's world, yes. In a true sense, no.)

And if you are afraid that you won't be pushed hard enough if you are too easy on yourself, don't worry, the rest of the world will gladly shove you.

Let us all practice being more patient with ourselves. You can start by giving yourself a great pat on the back. Good work so far! You are doing your best from your awareness level, and life just is what it is. If you are not where you thought you would be by now, let yourself be. It will come. With a newfound care and encouragement, you will most likely get there sooner. But who's counting? If you always find a way to enjoy where you are, you will not be in a hurry to get somewhere else.

Mindfulness Attitude: Non-Striving

Just hearing "non-striving" as in "not to strive" and "not to try for something" probably makes your business skin crawl. This is impossible! And you're right. If there is actually no striving what-so-ever, no willingness to move forward with your business, you will not do well.

But this mindfulness attitude can still be helpful and effective. Non-striving can point you to a sustainable meditation practice. Non-striving can also help to translate to the business world as an *awake* or *aware* type of striving. Both point to the importance of stillness and slowing down. As much as we loathe those terms in business, they are deeply useful.

In order to keep up with your crazy-beneficial meditation practice, it is in the slowing down, in the stillness of yourself, that you will find the real juice. That's where it works and how it works. If you constantly strive forward, forward, forward, you will find a million excuses to skip your meditation practice. And that's how you miss out on a clearer head, a mind less likely to wander and less likely to make mistakes, a better immune system and a healed nervous system—and your brain will not build more gray matter and make new neural connections either. As such, it's okay to stop sometimes in order to move forward. Actually, it's necessary.

When we are aware in our striving, we wait a beat, and we create a little gap between where we are and where we are striving to go. In doing so, we leave space for recognizing whether we're heading in the right direction and if we're heading there for the right reasons. It doesn't matter how fast you're running if you're running in the wrong direction. Much like running to a place you don't want to go is a waste of everyone's efforts.

Slowing down sounds so… slow. But almost everything becomes better from slowing down and being present. Better food experience? Slow down, and be present. Better kiss? Slow down, and be present. Better relationships? Slow down, and be present. Better golf game? Slow down, and be present. Now it's up to you to figure out how you can create better business.

Observe yourself and those around you being completely caught up in modes of doing, getting and wanting. That's all we do: do, do, do. And everyone who sits down and relaxes is either a lazy bastard or annoyingly accomplished. *The nerve! Sitting down and relaxing!* I have found that this is true for so many people, both at work and with our families. But if we can't find time to occasionally relax at work or with our family, what other time is there? The commute? That's hijacked by us being constantly annoyed at other idiots in traffic who are, clearly, not doing the right thing! This doing-mode as a default is not healthy. You need to slow down at times, stop at times, and feel that you are with yourself. There is so much more to you than just doing.

Ironically, doing much to get a lot done leaves you ill equipped to doing things with a clear head and a well-functioning body.

Have you ever heard of an airplane that just keeps flying? Me neither. The plane has to come down for fuel, stand still, and get checked out. If it didn't ever come down and, let's say, got fuel in the air somehow (if we are continuing with this analogy, this would be a pretty accurate description of how we are treating our bodily systems. Eating on the go, anyone?), there are still so many other functions that need to be taken care of in the plane. We have a lot more machine specific issues of course, but also those relating to making sure communication works with other flyers and giving all these people who help the plane fly a well-deserved break. We can push all these functions and people all we want, but we know what's eventually going to happen—we'll crash.

You, my friend, are a much more sophisticated machine than an airplane. Although it still puzzles me how these big-butted planes can fly, your body-mind-soul system intrigues me a hell of a lot more. Flying's got nothing on you, because you can soar and change the world.

So don't get carried away in measuring yourself—and others—by the results of what your "doing" produces. You have a right to just be. And as you let yourself slow down, you will notice how your presence alone, without any doing, can make a huge impact in a room and in the world. The best doing will unfold from your true being.

Don't equate your self-worth with how well you do things in life.
You aren't what you do. If you are what you do, then
when you don't... you aren't.
—Dr. Wayne Dyer

The next time you get caught up in the result of a task, instead of asking yourself *what*, ask yourself *how*. How you do things will have a far greater impact on your kids, your staff and your community than the exact what. As you bring awareness to your own vision of "how," there are parts within you that I bet would be delighted to have a conversation with you.

May I suggest you start with your heart?

The Briefing on FOCUS

- **In a world of omnipotent distractions, your ability to focus will be one of the biggest factors in determining your business (and otherwise) success. If you don't know what to focus on or how to focus, you'll never be a great leader.**

- **Focus requires clarity and discipline. It's not a job for someone with a poor-me attitude.**

- **You know what to focus on when you know what excites you, what your umbrella purpose (above your ego) consists of, what's important to you, when you know that you're here to serve; that you're not a victim and that whatever you need is available to you (not your ego). Also, that multitasking renders you ineffective.**

- **Whatever you focus on takes increased space in your life. This is the way you create your own life, based on where you put your intellectual and emotional focus. What do you focus on; victimhood or victory?**

- **Only you can be you and only you should fix—or can fix—your life. Bummer and blessing.**

- Our lives can be viewed as a constant battle between Mr. Autopilot and the Alive You. If you're like most of us, you let your mind wander and the autopilot take over more than half of your awaken time. You're literally missing out on your life. And then you die.

- The reason meditation works is that we train our minds to be fully aware in the areas where our bodies and minds are the most automatic. Namely? Breathing and moving. With that, we grow increasingly aware of our autopilot in real life.

- Since you make your own reality through your own perception, whatever you're thinking is always right to you, because you want to be right and you will make yourself right. With that in mind, what do you want to be right about?

- With a skilled mind, we focus on that which we want to have more of in life, and more of what we want shows up. What we don't want becomes a guide to steering our focus to what we do want, instead of getting stuck in continuing to focus on the unwanted things that, inevitably, will bring us more of what we don't want. (That should make sense.)

- Unfortunately, we can't foolproof our lives against disasters. But, the good news is, when disasters hit, big or small, we can choose how we think about them. Here's a good mantra for upsetting situations: "Choose a new thought. Choose a thought that feels better." Whatever makes you suffer in your own disaster, it's your disaster, and you can choose how to think of it. The faster you find a better feeling place within yourself, the sooner you can rise up, see clearly what needs to be done and be the leader that the rest of us need.

- A great way of having a meaningless life until the time of your death, with nothing really to show for it, is to never focus on anything that matters to you. Better yet, don't even find out what you passionately want to contribute with in the world. Simply distract yourself until your time has come to meet your maker; between Facebook and family drama, you will never run out of distractions. Yay! (Not really).

- Or, you can take charge of your glorious focus and turn that laser beam towards your meaningful passions.

FOCUS – Mind-Training Exercise

Write down a situation that you instantly thought of as a disaster—and that turned out to be a blessing in disguise.

This is what happened:
Notes:

This is my disaster scenario of the results:
Notes:

These were the actual results:
Notes:

FOCUS – Meditation Practice

With a body scan, we will practice Focus by using the sensation of our bodies as our anchor. With this kind of training, we can easily learn how to utilize our bodies (that we always carry with us!) to help us focus in our oh-so-distracted lives.

Body Scan: 5-15 minutes

Sit on a chair in a relaxed but alert position—your feet on the ground, your back straight but not strained, your head free from support, your hands resting on your thighs. Close your eyes.

Start by feeling your feet to the ground. The meeting place between your feet and the floor. Become aware of the surface that touches the floor. Make a connection with that awareness. And, without moving your toes, bring your awareness to the space between your toes. One space after another. Don't hurry. Once you have connected to the space between two toes, move on to the next space. Continue sensing the whole foot as you move your awareness through your calves, to your knees. Rest in the awareness of your body, right there. Feel the touching surface of your thighs as your hands rest on them. And your butt sitting on the chair. Feel the weight of you on the surface of the chair, just in the meeting place between you and the chair. That is where your awareness rests in this moment. Follow with your awareness up your spine, where the back meets the back of the chair, up through your neck, the top of your head, your eyelids, your ears, your jaws. Your awareness is slowly making its way down your shoulders, your arms, through your hands ... and you rest in the meeting of your hands and your thighs. There you are. Thank you.

When you are ready to come out of your meditative state, be careful in how fast you start moving about. Take your time opening you eyes, and feel what the body needs—a few stretches, a big yawn, to sit and stare for a while? Be sensitive to you. Enjoy feeling relaxed and rejuvenated, as you start moving about with the rest of your day.

Add-On Meditation Trick

The fastest way I know to connect with myself when I literally have no time, is to consciously connect with my feet. This is especially effective before a meeting or something that requires my full attention, and I feel a little scattered.

Meditation Quick Fix: 1 minute

As you stand or sit, plant your feet on the ground. If you can take your shoes off, great; if not, we'll work with what we've got. Close your eyes, if you can, and focus all your attention on your feet. The meeting place between your feet and the floor is a great place to which to anchor your attention. If your toes or the space between your toes is easier for you, please use that space as your anchor. Just be in this space for as long as time permits. If you only have one minute, that's what you will do. Let the thoughts that wander disappear like clouds, and come back with your focus to your feet anchors. Before you finish (which may only be after one minute), thank your feet for carrying you all day. If I were my feet, I'd be very happy for that recognition.

Trusting The Rain

As the nasty lawsuits from my divorce were over and won, I was left in a pile of debris that resembled those photos from Hurricane Katrina. I was exhausted after months of horrendous legal attacks and heavy learnings, and I was in a deep financial hole I wasn't sure I could claw myself (and my child) out of. On top of everything else, I needed to move out of my apartment. As a single parent, I'd never felt so alone. And it was right there, in the middle of the shattered space called my life, feeling weak and exhausted, having no idea how things would work out, that I had a surprising experience of what constitutes my power.

My daughter and I were only moving eleven floors up in the same building. The whole apartment, nevertheless, needed to be packed up and everything moved. And, as anyone who has moved a home knows, it doesn't really matter how far you're going. It's a big job.

On the day of the move, I had the elevators booked until 5pm and was almost done packing by the time I had to take my daughter to school in the morning. The movers were supposed to start as soon as I came back, but when I was ready to literally get moving, they weren't there. Where are you guys? I called and inquired. *Oh, we can't make it until 4.30.* The non-negotiable reality hit me like a ton of bricks. I only had one day overlapping between the apartments, and this was the day.

A mental fork in the road appeared. I saw such clear choices in front of me. I was exhausted, both physically and mentally, from the recent depositions, court appearances, interviews, emotional pain and sleepless nights, that I just wanted to lay down and cry. That was a choice. Because where on earth would I get the strength to do this on my own?

I was looking at the building-provided carts and what seemed like mountains of boxes and even more bric-a-brac that needed to be moved to an apartment I had no idea how I would be able to afford. What had I gotten myself into? What if I couldn't make it? Somehow, I managed to stop that particular direction of my thoughts before they got too far down that dark scary path. I could have chosen to count my painful body out, saying I could hardly lift a glass of water without excruciating pain. I could have chosen to think that this is where it ends; someone else is going to have to bail me out; physically, emotionally...

But I didn't. Instead, I took the situation in. I was experiencing just standing there in the debris after the storm and suddenly felt a deep sensation that, from here on, things would be fine. In fact, I felt that they could be absolutely great; that things could line up perfectly for me. It struck me that I knew how.

I remembered that, during the recent litigation hell storm, I had accessed a deep sense of strength, an unspeakable power within, on so many occasions. Although my worst nightmare had been a constant threat around the corner, I realized that there was peace to be had any time I managed to access the present moment. My thoughts of speculation and future nightmare scenarios in my mind had led me to feel unspeakable despair with emotions so painful that I sometimes couldn't stand up. Looking back at the process, I could see now how the sequences of my mind had worked; how I had felt bottomless despair; how I'd managed the abyss by staying in the present moment, and that it was from that peace in presence that I could access my power. It was a simple but powerful sequence that had kept my sanity. I had functioned as a loving mother, and I had prevailed.

Standing before my new piles of challenges, the idea of the power I had accessed through presence felt intriguing. I could sense how it always is possible for me to align with everyone and everything else, and that this alignment was just waiting for me to adjust, so that great solutions could fall into place. I realized that it was through presence that I would tap into a bigger awareness beyond myself, while allowing intention and trust to guide me. It felt like a specific instruction on how to reconnect with my power and a mental position that would turn my situation around. Awareness, intention and trust...

So life, in its usual capacity (or is it its humor?), in that moment, was testing my most doubtful spot. Between the three components, you see, the biggest challenge for me had always been to trust. Can I really trust that all will be well—that it actually already is well—and that life, ultimately, is good? And perhaps hardest of all—to trust that I am worthy of good things. How can life have awesomeness in store when so many experiences speak to the opposite? And who am I to be powerful anyway?

I had always had an easier time with both awareness and intention, but trust... Oy vey. This whole nightmare that had unraveled ever since I decided to leave my then husband a year and a half prior, had tested my trust and faith to the core. At every turn, trust was the theme. At every juncture, trust was the action of which I needed to remind myself to keep from falling apart. I needed to keep going then, and I needed to keep going now. The mechanics of the nightmare were over, but now I needed to build a completely new platform, far away from the professional comfort and familiar steadiness I had created in Sweden. I sure needed my power now—strength, energy, vigor—to create change and build anew. I just couldn't forget to trust, no matter how bleak things were looking.

I was eyeing the boxes, could smell the faint but specific cardboard smell and reasoned that my ability to trust (in life, in myself, in my power) had just been tested to the core of what a mother can bear. And it had worked. I had seen the sequence. I could do it again. I took my aching little body and got to it.

That was what life was offering right then and I chose to say yes.

I lifted and schlepped, packed and stacked, and made what must have been 30 rounds between the floors. It took all day, and I had to call a fellow parent from school and ask if she could pick my daughter up with her son and that I'd come to their place before long. I was lucky; she said yes. My painful hands were actually stronger than I thought, and I just kept going. I'm not saying that I *looked* gracious as I was puffing and schlepping, but at least I *felt* grace. By 4.30, the movers showed up, just as I only had the big pieces left. Good. I could pack up the essentials, and go get my daughter.

It was only a ten-block walk to my daughter's friend's house, but it was pouring rain. And not that kind of rain that can be coined romantic, no, no. This was the real New York downpour—relentlessly hard and completely horizontal—designed to get your underwear soaked. The umbrella I had brought was more like an inside-out joke than of any help, and before I completely lost my last thread of grace, I tossed it in a garbage bin, just as I had passed Lincoln Square.

I was so exhausted, realizing then that I was shaking from not having eaten all day and having lifted all that heavy stuff, pain everywhere, rain seeping in everywhere, thinking of the prolonged and painful legal process I had gone through, financial worries, and now this windy chilly rain that didn't even allow me to use an umbrella for shelter, and I just had to laugh. I looked up to the sky as the rain was pounding my face, opened up my arms and chest in an upward surrender, and asked out loud, *What else? You got anything more?*

I suddenly felt free.

In that very moment, I kid you not, the pocket of my seemingly ridiculous raincoat vibrated. I looked at my phone and saw a number I didn't recognize. I took shelter by the Biblical Museum on Broadway and answered the call. *Hi Linda, I'm just calling to say that you won the pitch! All the details aren't final yet. I just wanted to let you know that your proposal was right on target—really clear that you had listened to exactly what we need and come up with the best solutions. Congratulations!*

"Oh," I said, "What excellent news here in the rain, and I didn't even realize that it was a pitch!"

Are you kidding? You were up against two of the biggest design agencies in New York City, and you won! I'm happy for you. I gotta go, I just wanted to share the good news, and we'll talk more tomorrow.

I was dumbfounded as I used my wet shaky fingers to hang up the phone. Wow. So this is what it feels like to say yes on the inside, to trust, to find strength through the peace of the present moment, regardless of circumstance? Is this what it means to be aligned?

Knowing how I would be able to afford my new place was, of course, a huge relief. But, more importantly, I felt a pure and deep sense of interconnectedness with everything and everyone else in the world. I had trusted. Things had lined up. It was going to be okay.

> *Most powerful is he who has himself in his own power.*
> —Lucius Annaeus Seneca

In hindsight, it is interesting that I hadn't realized that I was involved in a pitch. It speaks so much to how power is partly fueled by intention, and, in this case, intention as purpose and integrity. I know why I'm in business. I know how I want to help people and what my integrity is made of. I had interviewed this prospective client so hard on what kind of product I was going to work with that I had missed the fact that I was up against fierce competition. I hadn't competed. I just did what I believed in and won. If red flags had waved for my integrity, I would have bowed out and still would have felt like a winner. That's powerful.

> *Most powerful is she who has herself in her own power.*
> —Linda Bjork, adapted from above

We have come to the third module: Power. Just hearing the word is titillating. Power. One of the most sought-after assets in the world. Probably the most misused word, notion and position as well. On the opposite sides of the definition of this word, we will find *Power as A Control Factor for Gain* and *Power as A Change-Agent for Good*. With awareness, you can choose which side of the scale you operate.

POWER AS A CONTROL FACTOR FOR GAIN	POWER AS A CHANGE-AGENT FOR GOOD

The power that is used for gaining or controlling is the power that comes from the ego. Unless you are seeking to be an unhappy and isolated person, I would steer clear from this power as much as possible. I am fully aware that this is so far the prevailing force in business. It doesn't mean, though, that there is anything of meaning to gain there, and it doesn't mean that you have to operate there. Just because other untrained minds choose that side doesn't mean you have to. This is why you have smarts and integrity. Use them!

The other kind of power, the power as a change-agent for good, is one that can be felt as energy and as interconnectedness that creates change. This is your true power. If you're going to be in business, why not use the kind of power that can move mountains? When you tap into this power, your innate power, you will be connected with the whole world and the joy of making a difference.

The good news is that your own true power is already within you, and you can find it through unconditional self-acceptance. "Hold your horses!" you say, "unconditional self-what?" Yeah, I know, I know, it sounds kind of—yikes—close to loving yourself unconditionally.

So, let's break it down in a nice long breath. And while you are breathing, let me tell you that my own journey from being impossibly hard on myself (and others) to taking leaps towards unconditional self-acceptance is living proof that there is hope for anyone willing to try. My favorite remedy for my un-willingness to tap into the greater good power is to laugh at myself. Life is just too funny to take too seriously, and I am way too goofy to be taken too seriously.

Above all, I feel great every time I remind myself to laugh at myself, to ease up on the serious pursuit of perfection. Because seriously? Perfection? - LOL!

So, where does this true power come from? Most of us are programmed to believe that even our inner strength is gained from the outside. Mostly from doing stuff that shows others and ourselves how powerful we are but also from having others give us power. A measurable concept, to be sure. With such beliefs, it may come across as a tad far-fetched that, after all my research and observations, it is abundantly clear to me that our power comes from the inside of us no matter what is going on outside; we are our own true power's power plant. *Could our power really be coming from somewhere that close after all the insurmountable efforts most of us go through to reach power in the outside world? Can so many of us really be barking up the wrong tree? Can it really be that simple?* Well, it wouldn't be the first time mankind complicates simple things, so bear with me.

Cultivate the kind of power
that no one can take away from you.

How do we cultivate inner power, and where do we start? I want to explore a few pointers on Power with you, all working as an extension of what we have shared in our INNER BUSINESS so far. With your foundation of knowing who you are (BEING), your ability to use your attention in a beneficial way (FOCUS), and your awareness of the workings of Mr. Ego and Mr. Autopilot, you will have a much better sense of what kind of power will serve you.

With a little work, you will see that you have access to a power, force and might that is way beyond what you have dared to imagine. Let's examine how to get there and turn our attention to the kind of power that no one can take away from you. No other power should be your focus. The titles and hierarchal badges can still be part of your life, as long as you don't identify with them. As long as you actually, and deeply, realize that all of that is not you. It may serve you to be in a certain position, and hopefully you have the chance to serve other people—and even the world at large—as well. But your position is not you. Let them strip away whatever they want because you will stand tall in what really constitutes your power; your true power, free from titles and appointed authority.

1. MIND-WHEEL
Getting Out of Your Own (Power) Way

**Nothing stands in the way of your own true power
as much as the exhausting thought-feeling wheel
that clutters your mind's capacity.**

Our first line of business is to learn how to control our overwhelming mind-spin of thoughts and feelings that don't serve us. If you're like most of us, this spinning mind sucks the living daylight out of your energy levels every day. Much like stress, awareness of our mind-spin is essential as a basic step in training our minds. If you don't know how to handle stress, there is not much personal development to be had—your system is constantly too stressed out to make use of your brain or other functions necessary for change. The same thing goes for your thought-feeling wheel in your mind. This mind-wheel of yours is so exhausting and brain-clogging that there is no power to be connected with unless this is taken care of.

So here we go. Starting with a snake story.

The Fake Snake

For as long as I can remember, the topic of power has fascinated me. As a daughter, a mom, a CEO, an employee, a waitress, an expert, a sister, a meditator and a woman, I have encountered most sides of the power coin. My thoughts have grown from fairly unaware mental notes in the schoolyard ("how come I lose my wind around that person but not around that person?") to pretty deep contemplations as a CEO ("where does my true power come from, and what constitutes it?").

In seeking answers, I've read quite a few (piles of) New Age, Psychology, and Mind, Body and Soul books, listened to countless audiobooks, and attended numerous lectures, seminars and workshops. Researching and learning continues to be a satisfying passion for a born scientist such as myself, and I can safely say that I am leading a much richer life because of it. And I seem to have stumbled upon some really profound answers.

In doing my research in the New Age shelves, I have to admit, there have been many moments when the credibility of this lofty community has made me rather suspicious. On some level, I've stopped asking the world to make sense, but I still appreciate when it does. As an example, my rational mind tends to react to recurring stories as they either bring value in their widespread understanding of the story or they simply make me question the authenticity of the messenger.

One story that keeps reoccurring in New Age literature and meditation groups is the one with the snake. It seems as though every other author and group leader in this community has been out in the desert (Where? In Sweden? Outside New York City?), and they have all wandered about in the desert heat and suddenly… stumbled upon a dangerous snake!

And, oh! How they have thought about how to get out of this terrible snake situation. Run or freeze? Oh, all the horrific scenarios that have gone through their minds. What if the snake bites? Is it poisonous? And yes, this has happened to all of them. And (spoiler alert), for everyone telling this story… the dangerous snake has turned out to be a rope all along!

The first time I heard the story I was like "Ah, okay, I get it; all those unnecessary thoughts of fear are exhausting, and how at closer examination things aren't what they necessarily seem anyway." Stay in the moment. Nonjudgment. Don't waste your energy on mind-made stories. Cool.

Now, the third, fourth and fifth time I heard the same story but from different people, I was getting increasingly annoyed. I didn't hear anything new, no new angle, nothing. Hey, it's a great message but if it's not your own true story, the message is certainly not heard because thoughts like *You are not trustworthy with your borrowed stories and silly sandals* echo much louder in my head.

So, just to share with all fake-snake-storytellers how much more fun it is to actually be authentic when making these possibly life-altering points, here is my own snake story.

I was just about to take a shower in a townhouse that I had recently bought in New York City, to be used as my home and office in the States. I had been the pushy driver behind this house purchase, whereas my partner (at the time) had sort of just let me go through with everything.

The scary thing about being the one who just pushes through with stuff is that if it all goes to shit, you're the one to blame. This time, there was quite a bit of money involved, plus I had looked at townhouses for only two days and then said *Yes! This is the one I want!* It simply felt right. Closed, signed and paid for in less than a month (which, for any non-New Yorker reading this, is lightning fast for The Big Apple).

So, there I am, in the townhouse I just bought on "feeling good about it," about to step into the shower when I see a huge disgusting spider. And not the regular NYC thing (which is gross enough), either. This one was truly large and was very hairy with what looked like hundreds of legs. I absolutely froze as my mind took a super leap; *F-U-C-K! The house has nasty bugs!* I was totally freaking out. *The walls must be filled to the brim with these disgusting fuckers, I can't pull the curtain—there will be an invasion of hairy spiders coming out of the drain. How can I sleep here tonight? Oh my God, I shouldn't have pushed for buying this house. New York City of all places, an infested rodent Mecca. I was too rash. Shit, how many years will it take to tear down the house and build a new one? And where will we live in the meantime?*

The one leg I was balancing on was fatigued by then so I had to move, and the hairy spider moved too. *Yiiikes! What a nightmare!! Somebody heeeelp! But hmmm... weird... It seems to move as I move... And it only moves when I move... Is it blowing in the draft my body is making? Is it... is it not a spider?*

I leaned forward towards it. Was it... It was... a lump of hair from my hairbrush! Exhausted, I thought of the snake story and jumped into the shower. Alone.

There. My story. Stay in the moment. Don't exhaust yourself with your mind-spin. If the snake and/or spider doesn't bite, you're fine.

The Mind-Wheel

Between the field of neuroscience and the personal development space, many with me would say that our thoughts are what generate our feelings. And although I personally believe that there are more complex programming and soul-connected fear mechanisms that fit into this puzzle, I find it immensely helpful to be aware of my thoughts as the primary cause of my feelings.

Your thoughts are the primary cause of your feelings.

In every situation we encounter, especially as we experience upset feelings, we can choose a thought that makes us feel better. If you ask Mr. Ego, this is B.S. because a lot of our negative emotions come from thoughts that he made up. But we can be in charge here, remember? As we learn how to choose a better feeling thought in any situation, we can calm our minds and slow down the spinning wheel all together.

A perfect example of how we unnecessarily exhaust ourselves from our spinning thoughts-feelings wheel is to look at what kind of assumptions we make about people and events, and how they make us feel. Just think how you feel when you react negatively to your own assumptions, which you made up in your head! (Duh!) A negative assumption is a negative thought and creates a negative feeling, and soon the spin cycle is in full speed. It's that simple.

Good news is, you can stop that mind-spin by catching your own negative assumption (which isn't true anyway because that's the nature of an assumption), which needs to happen as soon as the negative feeling creeps up. Your throat chokes and your blood is boiling as you assume that your employee is late because he (clearly!) doesn't respect you. Then it turns out that you had the time wrong. Or your stomach throws a rain dance as you assume that your boss' request for a one-on-one with you (with your luck!) will get fired. Turns out he needs a favor for the next big project. Your mind is not helpful like that. But your body is brilliant like that. It will tell you how you feel and, thereby, hint about what your thinking is doing. Whether it's a sinking feeing in the pit of your stomach, a wrench in your heart or a blow to the head, you will be advised: something's not feeling good! As you jump in, right there and then, and choose a better thought, you are suddenly in the driver's seat for experiencing better thoughts and better feelings. Think of the energy you'll save! (Worrying is a fruitless activity.)

When we believe in lies, we cannot see the truth,
so we make thousands of assumptions and we take them as truth.
One of the biggest assumptions we make is that
the lies we believe are the truth!
—Don Miguel Ruiz

I can't tell you how many times I have made assumptions about why a client is not calling me back after an important presentation. *Oh my God*, I start to mull, *they must not like any of the design concepts. They are such nice people, if they liked our stuff, they would have called by now. Shit, I should have thought of something bolder, she was wearing the newest Air Maxes with her suit, that's very bold. They probably want to go more Nike. Why didn't we make it sportier? And those hand-drawn icons – what was I thinking, that this is an art exhibition? They won't go for that. Perhaps I should call the client and just present some new ideas. I really need this account. In three weeks things are looking pretty empty. Shoot. I have to get the team together and be proactive about this. Let's see… idea number one…*

Phew! I get exhausted just thinking about these thought-monster-spirals that have happened far more often than I care to admit; every moment of which are completely useless. The only thing that happens is that I waste an enormous amount of energy worrying over something that more often than not turns out to be nothing. And if you really need your senses sharpened to detect and avoid danger, thought-clutter is your *worst* bet. The client calls back the next day and says that they have been on a company kick-off, love the stuff we presented and only have some minor changes before focus group testing.

> **I have lived a long life and had many troubles,**
> **most of which never happened.**
> —Mark Twain

Let's take the notion of a thought-feeling cycle back to your everyday leadership reality. Before you can lead or develop anything with ease and effectiveness, you need to bring awareness to your fears and negative emotions. However, most business people—in particular those who want to excel on the longitude of the career ladder—are hard-pressed to admit they are afraid. Of anything!

I have encountered many people (men) who, tense and hurried, say that they are not afraid at all; they just want everything to be done right. They don't have any negative emotions if you ask them; they just want everything the way they want them to be. Afraid of doing the wrong thing, anyone? Worried about the inevitable unknown about being a human being? Come on! If we are not being honest with ourselves, and if don't dare to be vulnerable, we're not going to get very far on our personal development trip, let alone have access to our innate power.

I say if you are not holy enlightened, you are partly (or wholly) in fear. That has to be okay to admit. I know I am at times. In fact, a quick test to see if you fear anything is to ask yourself if you ever have any negative emotions and/or if you ever talk to people in a way that you regret.

Yeah, I thought so. And for those of you who said no, you are either enlightened (hi Eckhart and Dala!), or you should check if you are a sociopath. We are human, after all.

How You Are Power

When we have learned to minimize the exhaustion from a spinning mind, we can train our minds to have access to our power at all times. We can one up ourselves and step into the notion that we *are* power. Think about it: you are power—as energy, as authority, as light, and as a change-agent for good.

- You *are* energy (everything is energy and energy is power).
- You *are* authority (you make all your decisions, including letting other people control you).
- You *are* light (the creative power that can outshine any darkness).
- You *are* a change-agent for good (as your power to act is one for a better world).

Your power undoubtedly resides in you, so why shouldn't you have access to it? If you take a moment to reflect, I'm sure that you will recall situations where you have found your own strength nothing short of amazing. (Ahem. Childbirth.) With some help from your mind, your heart and your body, something awe-inspiring has happened to you that made you connect with a core in you that can lift a mountain. Deep inside us, we can feel that unyielding power, especially as we are put to the test. We know we have it in us. Straighten your back, put your feet on the ground, and take a deep breath.

There. The inner room of awesome power is our starting point, our factory-made setting if you will. You always have access to this space.

Until you start messing with the door…

With the help of our fickle friends Mr. Stress, Mr. Ego and Mr. Autopilot, we have freely chosen to put a whole pile of garbage, used furniture and rusty bikes right in front of that inner door of power.

**What we put in our own way to prevent us
from accessing our inner power
is as stunning as the power itself.**

The pile is full of old stories and unforgiving thoughts. Here's where blame, self-pity and refusal to take responsibility add to our growing pile between us and our inherent power. We are telling ourselves snake and spider stories all day long, and we're exhausted. Our heads aren't doing us any favors here either, as our brains can't separate real threats from perceived ones (we get equally scared from a rope as we do a snake, if that's what our mind tells us is true). Our brains automatically fall back to narrative mode and will make up the most absurd stories in an effort to make sense of everything, including hairy spiders and torn-down buildings. No wonder we often feel powerless—we can't access the power room!

Start observing your thought-feeling wheel. Once you can recognize it, you will know how to change it. That's how you start connecting with your power and, in the process, have an available mind for life's important stuff.

2. SAYING YES ON THE INSIDE
Realizing Your Power Sequence

Most [people] rarely align with their true power, because it seems illogical to them that there is power in relaxation, in letting go, or in love or joy or bliss. Most people do not understand that their true power lies in releasing resistance— which is the only obstacle to their true power.
—Abraham Hicks

The keywords here are releasing resistance. Imagine yourself always saying Yes on the inside. That really means letting go of resistance. It does not mean saying yes to everything on the outside. In other words, I am not recommending that you say yes to everything that comes your way, which would generate some pretty crazy outcomes. This particular premise has already been explored in *Yes Man*, a movie starring Jim Carrey where he did just about anything including approving every single loan application at work, marrying a Persian woman over the internet, agreeing to be a bridesmaid and snorting Tabasco. So let's not go there.

When you say Yes on the inside (your acceptance of what is happening), it will release resistance. There, you have your power.

Can you even imagine yourself feeling complete and strong, in your full power, without comparing yourself to anyone or anything else? Can you imagine never reacting to any outside disturbances or opinions or circumstances? Can you imagine you just as you, powerful in your own right?

I'm not saying that this state of mind is achieved in an easy heartbeat—that's why we're practicing together. But what I am suggesting is that this is the mental space you want to be in. Speaking from one professional to another: this is where you will find the strength to make changes that really matter to you, which are aligned with your purpose, joy and vision. This is also where you will win new business. How can you not? As you stand in your own power, you can connect with the true needs of your prospects and access your brilliance to find the right solutions.

**Saying Yes on the inside has truly transformed
my way of preserving energy and power.**

Much like forgiveness, saying Yes on the inside does *not* mean that you agree with what is going on, endorse any wrongdoings, or let people off the hook. It just means that you make it easy on you. You skip the assumptions, the negative thoughts and the negative feelings. In other words, you make it possible for yourself to access your power by not making another garbage bag out of the shit that's going on around you. You don't pick anyone's trash up because you say Yes on the inside to what's going on. Yes, I see what you are doing and you can keep your trash. Yes, you are blowing a shit-storm my way, and I'm choosing to not absorb your attempts to cause damage. Yes, you are saying hurtful words, all the while I choose not to believe them. I know my truth.

As soon as you say No on the inside to the same situations (by not accepting that they're already happening), you are giving yourself a lot of unnecessary work. The ego will have a field day: You did not just say that to me?? How can you say that to *me*? How dare you do that to *ME*? The words suddenly seem real and will hurt you deeply. The actions that seemed hurtful now generate thoughts of immediate retaliation, as you get increasingly upset from arguing with what is already a reality. And if you actually think you can change people by giving them an upset piece of your mind, you are completely off the mark. Instead, say Yes on the inside. People do shitty things sometimes. Fact. Save your energy, and skip right to the solutions.

The True Power Formula

The garbage is out of the way and you are ready for the formula that will connect you with your awesome natural power. It is an interconnected sequence of events:

Listening + Alignment + Motion = True Power

- In order to tap into that real roar inside you, you have to start in stillness, to actually listen beyond the chatter of the world (beyond all the stories that your narrative mind puts together from life's overwhelming bombardment of images and information). Although it may sound counterintuitive, you have to stop before you move ahead.

- Then, in order to welcome things to "line up for you," you need to align your various parts of you with yourself and yourself to the world (which follows a formula of awareness, intention, and trust).

- As a last event to the sequence, you need to put your power in motion—which is to say a lot more than "taking action."

Listening (Stillness)

When you get still with yourself, you give yourself the opportunity to listen in. The listening is not primarily a doing in this case. It is a *being* in stillness. We have explored meditation quite a bit in this book, and meditation is certainly one way of connecting with stillness. From that space of being in stillness, things will arise (all by themselves) that are worth paying attention to.

This is not, by the way, to say that the "things" will be intellectual information presented in a PowerPoint on a timeline. Your real power comes from the deep listening that is beyond mind-made concepts. You will experience things you may not be able to intellectually describe. Don't bother. Focus on what you become (which you already are) in the stillness as you see your life with the healthy distance of awareness. As you feel yourself and experience yourself, remember that your outside business will extend from your inner business. When it's time to make choices on the inside, choose the better. Choose the kinder, the joyous, the generous—all that you wish for your outer business.

And please don't get me wrong—saying that your outer business is a reflection of your inner business is not to say that all billionaires and celebrities sport enlightened insides. The outer world does not have the power to change your inner business. Only you do—through your inner business and your own free will. You can have all the money and stuff in the world and be miserable as hell. In fact, many very well-off people are anxiety ridden and depressed. There are even psychologists with this kind of expertise! And no wonder they are miserable: The emptiness and utter feeling of being robbed of happiness is deep as hell when you have "gotten it all" and don't feel any better on the inside. Now all there is to do is to manage suspicion of people, security issues, and law suits from Satan and his grandmother.

The unyielding power we are talking about here is one that you only can access within you. It has to start in you. Get the Porsche by all means. Just do it independently of thinking that it has anything to do with your power. And don't forget that you can be as happy on a bicycle. But you can't be as happy on a bike if you choose such thoughts as, "I can't believe I'm still riding this freakin' bike to work—what a failure I am." The happiness aspect is up to you. By the same token, you can get caught up in traffic stress in your Porsche, getting enraged at the other idiot drivers while you yell at your boyfriend on the speakerphone. It's up to you.

You have the power to change your life.
The process starts with listening to yourself in stillness.

Listening to yourself in stillness is always number one and the point you will get back to in your ongoing quest of clearing the clutter between you and your innate power. And please don't take my word for it, just start creating space for yourself by being in stillness on a daily basis.

When you listen in stillness, you get clear on a lot of things. You notice what is important to you and what is just mind chatter that has nothing to do with who you are or what you want to be in this world. This is the stillness you reach in meditation. As I mentioned before (which is worth repeating often): In meditation, you learn how to pay attention to yourself in life with a little healthy distance between what's you and what's going on in your life. They are two different things. Add to that your increased ability of staying present, from the sheer practice of coming back to presence in stillness, and this listening thing starts to sound kind of cool, no?

I had a daily meditation practice long before it was proven effective to aid a host of mental, emotional and health-related issues. When I started, mid-nineties, they couldn't measure thought activity the way they can now, nor prove how meditation increases gray matter in the brain. I would never be writing this book, nor would I have introduced meditation to my staff (on company time and my dime) if I didn't "know"—in other words, if I hadn't experienced the benefits of meditation myself. It started with a leap of faith, a curiosity and a hunch. It has continued for two decades because it has continuously showed me spaciousness and grace I couldn't even have imagined in myself.

Alignment (Awareness + Intention + Trust)

The alignment we're exploring for your inner power to shine is one that comes to pass with awareness. A kind of flow that makes pieces to your puzzle line up... where you suddenly see a way where you thought there wasn't a way... where you find strength that you didn't think you had.

Since the word *awareness* is frequently used in intellectual contexts, let me remind you that the awareness that we are exploring here is not the one where you need to know everything. This is the kind of awareness that you experience beyond your thinking mind. Where you have a sense of yourself without labels and can feel purpose as you are with yourself, as you meet other people and as you move around in the world.

The awareness I am talking about, as a result from your listening in stillness and training your mind, is not perhaps what you are familiar with. I'm not talking about the kind that is used in breast cancer awareness or with the awareness of the wars in the Middle East. I am not referring to an intellectual awareness at all. In other words, to "live in greater awareness" is not to stuff your head full with more information. This deeper awareness we are getting to here is consciousness—the kind of awareness that can reach far beyond yourself into a universal consciousness of sorts.

You know that sensation we have talked about where most of us can sense an intelligence far beyond our own? Many people—myself included once upon a time—want to have a logical explanation to everything. If shit ain't backed by science, we won't listen attitude. But here's my take on it: As long as science can't explain where thoughts come from, I have to take in other advisors. The grandness of life just seems too exciting to miss out on, and a leap of faith in that mighty force that grows our fingernails and urges people to develop suddenly makes sense.

How about you? Are you really going to let science, a field that has been so dead wrong about so many things, dictate your world? What if your own sense of awareness is much closer to the truth?

> *Awareness is the power that is concealed*
> *within the present moment. ...The ultimate purpose*
> *of human existence, which is to say, your purpose,*
> *is to bring that power into this world.*
> —Eckhart Tolle

In order for powerful things to line up for you, awareness is the overarching key. If it helps, you can think about it as maturity. I love maturity! It is the ultimate meeting of awareness and experience. There. That's the mother of things lining up. As a mature being, you will skip all the nonsense that would steer you elsewhere and mess up the beautifully orchestrated lineup that is waiting for you. As an aware being, you can see beyond the obvious and always find a way to connect with power through the present moment.

Maturity = Awareness + Experience

Another big component of this alignment is intention. You need to be clear about what your intention is. I'm sure you've heard it many times; to reach a goal you have to know exactly what you want. I agree that it is true to some degree, but this is also a statement that is easy to misinterpret. If you think that you need to know exactly what you want and exactly how to get there and exactly what should happen for you to get it, you are not heading down a productive or healthy path. When you walk with those ideas of knowing everything, you will invite way too much stress to your system; you will feel tense as you have to guard the process to match your exact way and you will feel frustrated as evidence will start to emerge that things are, in fact, not always going exactly your way. You are left tense and frustrated, which we all know is not a good recipe for having awesomeness flow.

Choose, instead, to place your mind on your intention. What is your intention with this thing or scenario that you really want? When you upgrade your mind to focusing on the intention rather than the exact details, you will be free to see that there are many ways to have your intention come to fruition, and you will be open to the opportunities ahead. In metaphysics, this is also the only way that the universal intelligence will be able to come to your aid. Take it or leave it.

There is immense power that comes from the intention found in purpose. With a relaxed intention that lines up with what you've been getting in your listening in stillness, thoughts will be pure. That intention will come from your true self. See how the stillness and listening has to come first? How else would you know the truth of your intention?

There is another drive in you that you can choose the same word for—*intention*—that comes from your ego. You will know that it's your ego as your intention will feel tense, contracted, and perhaps even be so obvious that you wish for other people to lose in order for you to win.

Let's, yet again, steer clear, because your true intention will upgrade the quality of your life and serve as your best guiding star for your actions while affording complete openness to the details. No more small stuff to sweat. Hallelujah.

Be grateful for the abilities you've been given and the goods you've accumulated, but give all the credit to

> *the power of intention, which brought you into existence and*
> *which you're a materialized part of.*
> —Dr. Wayne Dyer

Another ingredient in getting to a place of alignment is trust. I know we've talked about trust before—how trust has been an area of great trials and tribulations for me, and how trust is a commonly explored pointer in many leadership scenarios. In fact, trust is as a word that is frequently used in any and all contents of relationships. It's a foundation for marriages, friendships, business partnerships, and so on. So, it shouldn't come as a shocker that it is also the foundation of your inner business; that it is just as an important ingredient in your relationship with yourself.

This inner trust has to do with daring to trust life, again—trusting that life is ultimately good and that there is a power within you that is beyond you.

As I recall personal travesties that have happened in my life, I see now that some of them were the best things that could ever have happened. I didn't see it at the time; all I felt at the time was the pain of not having it my way. I was in pain, and I was wrong.

I remind myself of this as I encounter more things in life that are not according to my plans. How do I know that what is happening right now shouldn't be happening right now? How do I know that what is happening right now is even a bad thing for me? How do I know that what is happening right now is not the best thing for me? How do I feel when I trust that all is well? How do I feel when I trust that I can accept things for what they are? How do I feel when I trust myself and my ability to be loving and kind?

With your increased ability to be present—the prerequisite for being aware—you will notice when opportunities come your way. This is actually how luck is defined: Preparedness meets opportunity. And you'll have them!

Luck = Preparedness + Opportunity

With Mother Awareness and siblings Intention and Trust, watch things align to your benefit; as you get still, clear, aware and focused, watch the pieces of your road line up for your joyride. Being still doesn't mean having a life void of doing. Quite the opposite can be true. Your marching with awareness, intention and trust might be the most powerful thing you can do. When you trust and have a higher goal, your doing will be in flow, if you let it. Without your resistance, watch how a subtle sense of deep power and favor rolls out.

Motion

Now, in the True Power formula, after Listening and Alignment, we have Motion. There is great power in motion. The real nifty thing about motion is that it creates new motion, powered by its own motion, also known as momentum. This is true both in the physical world and in the world of our minds. We love momentum—if it's one that serves us…

Power is often associated with doing. *I did that! I made it happen! Look what we made!* And rightly so. Sitting around doing nothing will not change much.

To use power to make change is one of its core ideas. If we are going to use our power in the right way, however, taking action is a cue for bringing in awareness and intention. In order for us to ensure that we don't end up on the wrong side of the power slide (gaining and controlling) we need to reflect before we take action.

There's a relentless cheer from performance coaches to TAKE ACTION! "If you can, you must," and other must-urbation messages. Unfortunately, this is doing most leaders a disservice. As leaders, we are already heavily weighed by dos and musts every single day. All eyes are on us to make things *happen*. What no one is giving us is the space to stop before we start. And that's fine because that is our job, not theirs. That's why our inclination to take action needs to be preceded by an encouragement to slow down, connect with ourselves, our awareness and our true intention before moving ahead. We need reminders to lean back before we lean in. We need reminders to take a breather before we take action.

Just to get things straight here: I'm an action-oriented person, who's never been afraid of rolling up my sleeves. If I didn't have a bed and no money to buy one, I'd build one. When a prospective client for my web design start-up in the nineties asked if I could make her site in a new program called Flash, I said yes. I read the daunting Flash instruction bible cover to cover in two days and built her site the following week. My point is, I'm a friend of action and would not advise you to stop before you go if there was no merit to it.

But there really is a thought-through reason as to why Motion (action) is the last part of the true power sequence for letting things line up for you.

See, action for action's sake is a personal invitation to Mr. Ego and Mr. Autopilot. Shortly after they arrive, they will be joined by Mr. Stress. They can't *not* jump on the word action. That's their cue. So, I made sure the sequence is in the right order so that you haven't invited them by mistake and, for extra precaution, I have renamed action, *motion*.

For those of you who jump to the finishing line too soon or run around like chickens with your heads cut off (although an image of a great black-Friday sale is actually more prevalent in my mind), *motion* is a reminder to bring awareness to your actions.

For those of you who never get off the couch (and who may even hide behind New Age affirmations as an excuse to be completely inactive), the motion pointer reminds you to move. A higher power (or anyone else) can't do much for you if you don't have any movement to start the momentum working off of. Connect with yourself, and get off the couch.

> *If one advances confidently in the direction of one's dreams, and endeavors to live the life which one has imagined, one will meet with a success unexpected in common hours.*
> —Henry David Thoreau

When you have listened with stillness, and when you have aligned yourself with awareness, intention and trust, you are ready to start moving towards your dreams. This is your power. And it is mighty.

3. SAYING NO ON THE OUTSIDE

Cleaning Up Power Suckers

What do you brag about? It may seem like a strange question, but seriously, what do you brag about? What do you hold as your badge of honor? This could be a helpful indicator of power drainage. Because if it's how much you work, how little you sleep, how fast you run, how sick your are, how busy you are, how much you have to travel each week, how terrible your boss/wife/teenager is, or how many all-nighters you pulled last month (oh yeah, "I have it worse than you" apparently gives full bragging rights)... you are in trouble. And with trouble I mean that you are not going to become very powerful anytime soon.

As long as what you hold out about yourself for the world to see is ego-based, fear-based, or I-can-take-a-better-beating-based, you are giving your power away. You are awesome. Start bragging about that instead.

It almost seems ironic. We were born with pure powerful souls under immensely magical circumstances that conspired to make this seemingly impossible blessing called life come to being. Then we grow up and choose to live our lives scared and small. Even as well-adjusted middle managers with roofs over our heads and 401k's under our mattresses, we are often scared, or we become "powerful" by making other people feel scared and small.

The disappointments and setbacks we encounter along our journey make us forget about our true power and true potential. We have let the spiral of thoughts, feelings and beliefs muffle our power to a point where we barely have enough energy to drag ourselves through the musts of our lives. This is no way to live. It's not even a remote version of the way to live.

Two things I know:
In the core of our beings, we are powerful beyond measure, and;
We can change the world to something much more beautiful
than when we came here.

So, let's examine some of the concepts that suck your power and make a change for a more powerful you.

Here are a few power suckers to explore and start cleaning up:
1. Believing that you are a victim
2. Negative self-talk
3. Making excuses
4. Turning outside for power
5. Trying to control other people
6. Competing with others (on an ego-level)
7. Engaging in judgmental speculation
8. Hanging out with other power suckers

Believing That You Are A Victim

Every one of us is challenged with victimhood. That is just part of being human and the basis of our archetypical existence. You may not identify with being a victim, but the truth is, if you ever blame anyone or anything, you are acting like a victim.

Believing that you are a victim will
suck your power right out of you.

Life will continue to present situations where your sense of victimhood is challenged—that's a given—the question is, what will your attitude towards it be? In other words, it's not a question of *if* you will face hardships that test the core of your being but *when*. And, as a leader, you have signed up for plenty. It's the nature of the beast.

So, what will happen when life puts a little pressure on you? Or a lot? Do you fall into the powerless trap of being a victim (including passing blame), or do you recognize that you can always choose victory in you?

Anything (and I mean anything) that happens to you
is an opportunity to see how you can be victorious.

Here's a sobering truth: Whatever you and I face in our lives, it will never be as gruesome as what the Holocaust survivor and neuroscientist Viktor Frankl experienced in the Nazi death camps. He wrote:

> *What was really needed was a fundamental change in our attitude toward life. We had to learn ourselves and, furthermore, we had to teach the despairing men, that it did no really matter what we expected from life, but rather what life expected from us. We needed to stop asking about the meaning of life, and instead think of ourselves as those who were being questioned by life—daily and hourly.*

Life will question you. Life will expect from you what you think you cannot give. But you can. If Victor Frankl could, you can.

The moment you start pointing fingers and believing that your happiness is for someone else to provide, you will not make it. They may be wrong, but you are not a victim. They may be horrible, but you are not a victim. You can only be a victim inside yourself. This is how the choice is yours. If you do not believe that you are a victim, you are not.

The power you feel in yourself when you refuse to let any person, any collective, or any situation dictate how you feel, is immense. Start by vowing to yourself to never blame anyone—including your parents, your boss, or any event from the past—for the perceived shortcomings in your life right now. You have everything you need.

You are far from a victim.

You are powerful beyond belief.

Negative Self-Talk

In an incessant manner, most of us are involved in some pretty harsh negative self-talk. *No wonder you blew it. You suck. You were never that smart anyway. Who are you to think that you deserve this? You're fat.*

If you heard someone talk to a friend like that, you would be quite upset. You'd likely wanna smack 'em in the face and say How dare you? Well, how dare we talk to ourselves in such derogatory terms? Time and time again, we cut ourselves down at the ankles as we try to move along on our path of power. We know too well that we will not be good leaders or make a great impact in the world if we keep getting stuck in negative feelings. It seems like our negative self-talk is trying to drown out our omnipotent feeling that we are not worthy of the good that is coming our way, the good that we already are.

**Negative self-talk is a sure way
to make yourself lose your power.**

More famous than Marianne Williamson herself is a quote of hers that made quite a dent in the world when Nelson Mandela delivered it in his Inauguration Speech in 1994. The quote sure is inspiring for easing up on our self-berating messages and stepping into our power:

> *Our deepest fear is not that we are inadequate. Our deepest fear is that we are powerful beyond measure. It is our light, not our darkness, that most frightens us. We ask ourselves, Who am I to be brilliant, gorgeous, talented, fabulous? Actually, who are you not to be? You are a child of God. Your playing small does not serve the world. There is nothing enlightened about shrinking so that other people won't feel insecure around you. We are all meant to shine, as children do. We were born to make manifest the glory of God that is within us. It's not just in some of us; it's in everyone. And as we let our own light shine, we unconsciously give other people permission to do the same. As we are liberated from our own fear, our presence automatically liberates others.*

You will not have access to your own power if you keep putting yourself down. Effectively, you can't even help anyone else become a great leader until you tap into your power.

You are indeed a fabulous person meant for greatness. You have a bigger mission in life. As you feel why you are here and the higher you lift your gaze, I hope that you find it less interesting to beat yourself up over your favorite shortcomings. It happens to me often. By habit, I put myself down with my usual suspects. Then I remind myself. I am here in the world full of people who I am open and willing to help, should they let me—and a whole array of things that I may have been insecure about suddenly seem unimportant. What does it matter if the cool people think I'm corny if I help someone? I am corny!

Whatever drives the universal consciousness forward has a place for each and every one of us. You are still here. If you weren't supposed to be here, you wouldn't be. Stop beating yourself up over details. Go and be awesome instead, now that you're here. Why not? Before long, you won't be.

Making Excuses

We may *say* that we want to be powerful, that we want to connect with our inner strength to make a positive change in the world. But then... Well, it takes a little work. It's not that it's harder to be in a powerful position within our self than to be in a weakened state, but it's different. And we don't necessarily like different. We have to call upon things like courage, integrity, acceptance, kindness and humility. We even have to have a good attitude. And that's where quite a few decide to jump off the wagon...

We are so used to making excuses that keep us from reaching our full potential and fulfill our purpose. It's automatic and comfortable, thank you very much. And I understand it's scary. We're so brilliant and powerful that, putting aside the good nature of true power, it's easy to be intimidated. We may even have a few relationships that would have a different dynamic if we were strong.

I used to be petrified speaking in front of a group, let alone an audience. I was so nervous that my whole body would shake and my voice would turn weird and, as I experienced my own weirdness with all these people looking at me, I would completely lose my footing. Ironically, I now make a living speaking in front of audiences. My bet is that most people who see me on stage would never have guessed that this situation would make me faint beyond functioning in the past. Believe you me, I would make one excuse after another to not have to deliver anything in front of a group. Until the day I accepted that my desire to make a difference was greater than my fear. I sometimes still get nervous before delivering a speech, but it doesn't bother me as much now and, more importantly, it doesn't stop me from sharing important inspiration to the world.

What happens at work if you are no longer part of making yourself small? Are you ready to be seen and heard? What happens in your marriage if you are strong, happy and capable? Are you ready to have relationships that are built on a mutual want instead of a mutual need?

We keep finding excuses to not step into our full powers. Which ones are yours? What are the excuses with which you are constantly dragging yourself down? We are not in a blame mode here, so we are not even pointing fingers at others who may find plenty excuses (explanations of the truth if you ask them) to hold you down. Not everyone is ready to have you blossom and bloom in your mighty glory. And that's okay. That's your job. You are the one who can do you. You are lacking nothing.

You are anointed to be you. Nobody can beat you at being you.
You are fully loaded, totally equipped, uniquely designed,
for the race that has been laid out for you.
—Joel Osteen

As we engage in feeling offended, betrayed, abandoned, let down, or hurt, we keep ourselves from experiencing life as whole human beings. With our excuses lined up, we will not accomplish our dreams any time soon. We won't even be able to take steps in the right direction towards personal development, inner growth and freedom. Instead of putting in the effort that is required, we turn to our time-tested excuses. And if they don't work, we'll make up new ones.

For our own sense of feeling temporary dignity, we often engage in "if only, then" thoughts.

If only I get promoted, then I will be more confident.

If only my boss tells everybody how invaluable I am, then I can stand tall before her.

If only I get more likes on my Facebook page, then I will contact the publisher.

If only my paper gets published, then I will apply for the job.

If only he will call, then I will be happy.

The problem with the "if only, then" thinking, is that the time may never come, and it will never be enough. You can't get enough outside satisfaction to make you feel confident. Any confidence you gain from outside achievements can only be temporary and, if you hang your hat on them, are guaranteed to make you less powerful and less confident. You might as well start in the only time you ever have: right now. Anything else is just a poor excuse to not deal with your inner business and be part of making this a better world.

Here's the deal: If you don't have it, you don't need it. You have everything you need right now. Sure you can have other stuff and other circumstances later, but later is only a concept and nothing you know anything about. Right here and right now you have what you need. Except perhaps the right attitude about your excuse-making. Any excuse you have offers a solution. If you are ready, willing, and able to see that there is an opposite truth and a helpful reality to the excuse you are putting in your way, you are ready for your own power.

Turning Outside For Power

You already have all the power you need within you. Perhaps you feel it at times, or at least have an intellectual appreciation for the idea that our source of power could not possibly be on the outside. Yet, this is where most of us turn. There is something in our collective programming that makes us turn outward when we seek the feeling of power or confidence. Confirm me, feed me, adore me, identify me, praise me, love me…

Some of us turn to bigger cars, trophy partners, impressive titles, and plenty of people to boss around. Others make sure to snare those around them in emotional traps so that they can dominate the mental chess games. This is where the power-induced bosses completely missed the leadership train.

And then there are those of us who take the intellectual route. We learn to recite important passages of law, history, religion, or poetry and upgrade our vocabulary so that few understand. We'll be ready to win any argument, to one-up everyone in our wake.

Oh, and let's not forget those of us who find power by physical force, athletic or aesthetic. That's very popular. The prettiest, handsomest, biggest-boobed, skinniest, muscular, most luxury handbag, fastest runner wins. Now that's a sight for sore eyes.

Whatever route to power you choose, these are just different ways of metaphorically feeling like you have the tallest building in town. The one Mr. Ego wants you to build. Whatever the specifics and though you may think this pursuit of power is making you more grand, it's actually draining you of your real power. It's exhausting when you always have to be on guard, making sure that no one else is building a taller building than yours. Tending to your own building doesn't seem to do the trick in this fierce competitive reality where, in order to stave people off from obtaining power that you "should have," sabotaging them is the only effective way.

As long as you compare yourself to others, this tall building game is essential. It is a true battle of egos and it's exhausting. Even worse, as long as the battle is being run by Mr. Ego, you will never even be happy. Remember? Mr. Ego can never be happy. He can never be satisfied. You will never make the cut.

Thinking that your power comes from the outside is just another way of handing your power over to someone who couldn't care less.

Outside power is not the solution. Jim Carrey puts it best, "I wish everybody could get rich and famous and have everything they ever dreamed of, so they will know that it's not the answer."

No matter how we slice this dice, you will not find your real power on the outside or in your ego. It's just not going to happen. We aren't programmed to look in the right place and we haven't been taught how.

But it's time.

Here are two metaphorical pointers:

One: Key of Presence

As you turn your attention to your inner power door, chances are that you have some garbage sorting to do. You won't get access to the door as long as your piles of garbage are in the way. Guaranteed, your garbage will have thoughts and feelings of resentment. Here, we will find regret, blame and grievances. Part of your piles will also be some big bags of fear. These will include thoughts and feelings of worry, anxiety, stress and tension. With these bags, you will not get to the door. Your best bet for a clean-up service will be one of learning how to stay present, regardless of circumstance. Yes, regardless of circumstance. This is where you choose peace, you choose acceptance, and you choose joy. By choosing these formats of love, your garbage bags will dissolve.

Two: Door-hinge Direction

As the garbage is cleared enough and we're standing in front of our inner door to power, it's easy to believe that the door opens by pushing it open. Whatever we've been seeking is "out there," so we push outwards. We're pushing and pushing and pushing to get there. But the door won't budge. It's exhausting, and we lose more of our power. The moment we realize that the door to our inner power opens inwards, it will fling right open.

You don't have to try to change things on the outside to connect with your power. You're it already.

Take care of your garbage, open the door inwards, and connect with a power that can change the world.

Trying To Control Other People

What is true for you is true for everyone: You ultimately only decide over yourself. This is really annoying for business managers as it would be much more practical for the bottom-line if everyone just did what they were told.

Whether a person chooses to let programming and an unquestioned mind be the basis of her decision making or if she takes her steps with awareness and an expanded intelligence is up to her. Someone can also change over time, decide to do something else, go from bad to great or from good to worse. It sucks. But there it is. We can't ultimately control people. This is a terrible reality for a boss.

> *Life doesn't exhaust us.*
> *Trying to manage people does.*
> —Dr. Robert Holden

I'm sure you have already noticed that the more we try to control, the worse we do and the worse we feel. The more we hold up our leadership title card, the more we push people into flexing their own power card. You can't control me!

The real joke is on us when we, in an attempt to control people, get really angry with them. We try to exercise power over other people by screaming at them, all the while we are giving our power away to them by being angry.

I know that it *feels* like you are in command, even by having the right to raise your voice or having a tantrum aimed at someone. When people don't follow your instructions at work, even though you've told them a million times how if should be done... every time with your blood boiling... they're still not listening (bastards!)... and you raise your voice (and your blood pressure even more)... It doesn't make you powerful. It drains you. It can even kill you. Research shows that heart attacks are more likely to occur after an episode of intense anger. Who's the boss now?

Thinking that you are in control of people, or anything other than select parts of yourself for that matter, will always exhaust you. But only every time, so it's up to you if you want to give it a few more gos.

How do I know it will happen every time? Because as soon as you are trying to control people, your ego is effectively fighting with another ego. Be mindful of this power struggle—there's a lot of energy to be lost here. As soon as you dig your heels in, you are investing truckloads of your valuable power. There are times when it is fruitful and worth it to push something through, but never if you get blind-sided by your own ego.

You have to be more aware than your ego is strong. Your ability to inspire has to be greater than your appointed power of threatening with consequences (more on that in the SPARK chapter which follows this one). In the meantime, the bad news and the exceedingly good news is that you are only in charge of your own business.

Competing With Others on an Ego-Level

When you compete with others, you activate their egos. Any comparison can bring out the worst in someone. You may not think you're showing who's boss by passing comparative arguments and leaving no room for questions, but everyone can feel it. As soon as you activate other people's egos, you start wasting a lot of energy in the room. The ripple effects of these seemingly harmless situations will drain you of power—and that your teams.

Start an experiment, and be mindful on what kind of impact you have on other people. Observe yourself. You may think that your mission in the room is simple: You just want to get in and out as fast as possible—here's what you need to do - that's that - because I told you so. Or perhaps your style is different. You may think that your gentle demeanor is making everyone feel safe, all the while your careful approach is a cover-up for your lacking sense of value, and people can't wait to see what they can get away with next. In other words, the roles are switched but the ego-energy withstands.

Whatever it is, start observing. Whatever your idea about yourself and the impact you have on other people, start over. Start observing yourself anew. And start seeing others anew. If you combine this with a meditation practice, even if it means short exercises daily, your ability to observe yourself will increase rapidly. There is a lot for you to gain from this. As you start catching your own participation in ego-level competitions, you have the power to bow out.

If you want to develop your business and break new grounds, you have to understand how you can help people with your presence connected to power. Don't activate their egos! There is never a good time for you to beat anyone.

Shine plentiful, but not by turning other people's lights off.

Engaging in Judgmental Speculation

Oh, gossip (I just made the headline a little fancier)—a power player from the ego team that we mistakenly dismiss as relatively harmless. A lot of gossip is plain silly and is not meant to be taken seriously. After all, it's "just gossip."

Gossip seems to bond people over speculative oh's and revealing ah's, generating joint enemies ("us against them") in an attempt to make us feel more powerful.

Employee A: "Did you see the CMO? She's wearing that green blouse from H&M that was just on sale!"

Employee B: "I know. How can she wear that with those pants? She has no taste! Or maybe she's colorblind?"

Employee A: "All people in finance are colorblind; that's why they stick with gray. And I thought she made money?"

Employee B: "Well, I heard that her husband doesn't work."

Employee A: "He takes all the money, for sure. He probably has a gambling problem."

Employee B: "That would make sense with all those trips to Atlantic City. That's where he goes, right? What a travesty. She's hiding it well."

Employee A: "Except, of course, for that blouse."

The need for gossip seems ingrained in many people, especially for an untrained mind. It does not take much awareness though to recognize that it is the gossiper we should be wary of, rather than the stories told about the absentee person. When you're not there, you'll be talked about, too.

It doesn't take much maturity to realize that the effects of gossip can be absolutely devastating to people. Lives can be ruined and families broken apart. And that's the whole idea—for the gossiper to feel powerful. Speculating with this kind of judgment and callousness is yet another tool for the ego to have the tallest building in town; tearing down another's by the sheer force of a damaged reputation.

> ***Fire and swords are slow engines of destruction,***
> ***compared to the tongue of a Gossip.***
> —Richard Steele

As much as gossip can be devastating to the reputation of people, especially at the time when swords and engines were valuable references, there is an even worse form of judgmental speculation. It happens far too often in the most hard-to-catch and dangerous place. It's not on social media. It's in our minds. We are all losing precious power from the non-stop judgment our untrained minds are producing. Our judgments are robbing us blind of the experience of life! One judgmental speculation leads to another. And another. And another. And there we are, not living life, but having a spinning wheel for a mind judgingly speculating everything we do. And we're not being nice to ourselves!

The sooner you can catch yourself speculating, the better. If there is little or no joy attached to your speculation, just stop. You can do it. You can choose something else. A better feeling thought. As you do, be mindful and kind with your words, both to yourself and to others.

> *Choose your thoughts carefully. Keep what brings you peace,*
> *release what brings you suffering, and know that happiness*
> *is just a thought away.*
> —Nishan Panwar

Hanging out with other power suckers

If we jump straight to the punch line here, it would be the following: Stop hanging out with power suckers!

It's fascinating that we have so many people around us that suck our power, and yet we choose to stick around! No other point from the "cleaning up power suckers" list resonate so well across the board with my audiences as the power drainage we feel from hanging out with power suckers. We all know this point! And we all seem to have a hard time separating ourselves from them.

Ask yourself, why do you still have them around? Or perhaps more accurately put, why are you, as your suffering you, still around? In other words, there is an obvious choice for you to make: Either remove yourself from the situations with your power suckers, or change how you perceive them inside of you.

With a few people, removing yourself is possible. I say, go ahead. See, negativity breeds negativity. Even if you have your own ego at bay and a cheery attitude, being surrounded by power suckers will surely activate your ego (just give it some time). Before you know it, you'll be trying to tear down buildings again. Here's the big news: You don't have to hang out with all of them! You can love them at a distance. *Thank you and have a nice time with your inner hell over there*. You don't have social obligations to people who are draining your power. Unbelievably, this took me years to figure out.

Who drains your power that you are in a position to walk away from?

Now, we can't necessarily remove ourselves from everybody who drains us. If you can't, I say as step number one: Try to minimize your time spent with them. You need to protect your loving wellbeing, and there aren't that many social musts when you start living a life of taking full responsibility for yourself. But if you really can't completely remove the power suckers from your life (you might have one as a boss, one as an in-law, and another as a neighbor), you can still minimize your time with most of them. If you can't stand the party but have to be at the party, you show up and excuse yourself early. If you can't stand your new brother-in-law, don't go on a two-week cruise with him! If people you work with are bullshitting power drainers and you don't want to quit your job, then minimize any time possible with these people! You don't have to have lunch with everybody at work just because everybody else is. Skip lunch with them, start a meditation class over lunchtime, and get a healthy meal to eat by yourself.

What can you do to minimize time with your power drainers?

In order for us to have sustainable relationships—both to ourselves and to others—we can't be walking away from people as our *only* remedy. Some yes, others no. Either way, I don't want you to feel weakened by others. I want you to be independent of other people's opinions and joyous within you *regardless of circumstance*. You are the most challenged by power suckers when you feel out of balance. Good thing, then, that there are things you can do on the inside of you.

- Much of your power is generated from joy. As a general way of boosting your own power, you need to really start making time for yourself that brings you joy. And not as escapism and temporary relief, but for the long term. What really brings you joy? Go there often and generate some power.
- As you encounter power suckers, remind yourself that the more you release resistance, the more powerful you will feel. In other words,

the more you think about this underdeveloped idiot power sucker as a necessary evil in your life, the less powerful you'll feel. See the person without judgment. Just try it. And perhaps you'll be surprised to feel that you will be filled with love and kindness instead towards this person who, clearly, doesn't know better. If she did, she would stop.

- A third pointer with power suckers is to be aware of your own body. Just the way you stand and walk can be a great source of power. I often think of power as coming from the ground—that I am "stepping into" power. As I stand with both feet on the ground or walk while intently connecting to the ground, I allow for this strong flow to push through from my feet, up through my legs, my spine, and all the way up through my head. When I do that, something shifts in my stance and in my energy. I feel myself grounded. A space where power suckers have little effect on me.

**Steer your self towards power gaining
instead of power draining.**

The opposite of power draining is power gaining, and now you know how to protect yourself and train yourself to take care of the inside of you. Remember, walk away when you can and minimize time when you can.

4. BEYOND OUR INSIDES

What If There Is More Than This?

*The intuitive mind is a sacred gift and the rational mind
is a faithful servant. We have created a society that honors the
servant and has forgotten the gift.*
—Albert Einstein

Warning: This is not a section for everyone. Only those who are open to the idea that he or she may not be the ultimate King of the Hill can read this and get something out if it. Only someone who has already experienced (or at least had a convincing whiff of) how life-altering things sometimes come together in a fashion beyond human capacity, can hear this part. So if you're still afraid of the New Age bookstore, this is not for you. Not yet.

For whoever is ready, the truth is that when we are exploring the kind of power that cannot be taken from us, we have to examine what is real, what is not real, what is infinite, and what is finite. We cannot talk about what is real and infinite without doing some exploration of a higher intelligence in life.

This is not a section for Mr. Ego or any of his buddies who insist on living solely in his thinking mind. This is not a section for you if you believe that you're it, that the capacity to create stops with you, that there is no such thing as a sum being greater than its parts, that we live and die and that's that, that in the meantime we are all separate from one another, that there is no other purpose bigger than ourselves, that there are no invisible energy forces far beyond what meets the eye, and that there is really no point to this whole thing called life. Hey man, that's cool, not everyone can be open to a bigger universal mind and miracles. You can skip to page 199.

No seriously, skip to page 199.

For those of you still reading, awesome! Taking a leap of faith, whether it rings true to the exact words of your religion or non-religious beliefs, is a great mark of someone who has one of the most important qualities for having a good life: curiosity and willingness.

I am not going to pretend that I have cracked the code of what constitutes a higher power. And let me throw in the caveat, yet again, that this is not explored with any religious connotations. I do know, however, how much undefined energy forces have helped me far beyond my own capacity or any other abilities in the natural. While meditation has historically been a part of most religions as a contemplative worship, we use meditation without conversing with any particular god. What I can say with conviction is that meditation has helped me tremendously in this time-space continuum in which we live. It has helped me be a calmer, more considerate and much sharper human being. It has continuously healed my nervous system so that I can experience life in a connected and joyous way.

The same non-labeled experience goes for a higher helping force that I experience in my life. I am fully aware of the times, in and out of business, when there has been something larger at play. I have felt protected, encouraged and inspired. I have felt energy from unexplainable sources in impossible situations. I know what it feels like, I can feel the connection, and I know how to tap into it. But I don't know the ingredients—all I can offer are pointers on how to access it and share what my own faith in a universal intelligence has meant for my life and for my business.

Polls show that most Americans believe that human beings have a soul. Still, most people I encounter are sensitive to mentions of religion or even spirituality. I can understand that. I personally do not belong to any particular religion but certainly respect those who choose it. And I respect those who choose not to. Beliefs are beliefs, whether they are for or against.

I personally use the word spirituality in my life (oh the big s-word!), but to me, spirituality simply means unity. Oneness. That we all belong together on some level and that there is a universal bond between us and everything. What's important to me is that, religious or not, we learn to have a non-judgmental approach to people and situations we encounter. I'm not saying this is easy, but I do know that we are missing out on so much of life, just because we are discounting other people, especially with regards to their religious beliefs (or non-beliefs).

Non-believers are quick to look down on faithful people with an overtone of superiority a la *Oh poor mentally weak people who need an invisible friend in the sky to make them feel better.* But the joke will always be on them as long as they are judgmental.

A quick note, then, on the other side of this hot potato: Some religious people see themselves as the chosen ones. That they, by virtue of their blood lineage, are worth more that the rest of us as they have a special "in" with god. That's bound to piss the non-chosen people off. Of course! Try that sentiment in a schoolyard and feel the inevitable fist punch in your gut. I can feel empathy for people who have been chastised and humiliated, even tortured and killed, because of their religion. I can see how that would raise emotional and mental needs to believing that they are, in spite of (or perhaps because of) everything that is being done to them, special. Unfortunately, that makes the pendulum swing the other way.

The oppressed learn to oppress. Suspicion creates suspicion. Hate breeds more hate. We see it in cycles of numerous religions and cultures over time in the world. But, can we stop already? Is it possible for us all to just get off our high horses, our oppressed righteousness, and deep feelings of vengeance?

Can we all just say that misery has visited everyone at some point and that, the sooner we realize that we are all very, very, very similar to one another, the sooner we can call it quits?

I happened to be born in one of the safest countries in the world to two good-looking, hard-working Scandinavian parents. Jackpot. Especially as it is perceived. Listen, my genetic makeup is scary similar to that of a banana. I could have been the Chiquita you wolfed down this morning! There is never a moment, however, when I forget that I could have been born to any other parents or circumstance, anywhere in the world.

When we remind ourselves that we could have been any other person, openness and tolerance to other people arise. Seeing others as part of us, or at least part of our life experience, is essential to connecting with the energy field that links us all together.

> *We are like islands in the sea, separated on the surface*
> *but connected in the deep.*
> —William James

We really are extraordinary power packages, connected to a universal creative source. The way I experience it, I have some intelligences that are connected to me as a person. I don't want readers who chose to skip this chapter to miss this whole notion of intelligence mapping (more on that in the next chapter: SPARK), so here is a briefer description:

- I have an intellect with a logical type of intelligence.
- I also have a heart with an emotional, wise type of intelligence.
- I have a body, with a physical intelligence that informs me about so many things that are going on in my physical, mental and emotional systems.
- I also have a soul, with an extraordinarily deep intelligence that sees the vast picture and recognizes that I am connected to everyone else.
- To top it off, I experience an even deeper connection beyond my soul, as if my soul intelligence were hooked up to a larger universal mind: a higher intelligence that connects us all.

(I will stop here before it gets too weird, even for those of you who are still willing and curious.)

This is how we are all deeply connected. Through being humans and through being more than humans. If spirituality means anything to me as a word, it is that we are all connected... that we all are ultimately part of one buzzing energy field... one mind, that whatever we do impacts everyone else... that we are not separate from one another.

This is where we meet, recognizing that we are all in this together—that I could be you and you could be me. As we breathe in that notion, we can feel that I *am* you. You *are* me.

There is a deep reason to why we are here, if we choose to look at it that way—if we choose to see the bigger picture. There is even a deep reason to be in business, if we choose to look at it that way—if we choose to connect to the bigger picture.

Through my years as a CEO and as a meditation and mind-training teacher, I have met a surprising number of people who don't feel good about their work, at all! Even worse, they have accepted that dead feeling they've acquired as they've turned themselves off to cope with their tedious work life. Now, they perform the musts and tasks they are paid to do, but they don't feel alive. They don't have fun. They don't feel any meaning or purpose in their lives. Except, perhaps, providing for their families. The cruel trick is on them though, as their deadness from work prevent them from feeling alive and having fun with their friends, families and themselves.

> *The truth is, everything will be okay*
> *as soon as you are okay with everything.*
> *And that's the only time everything is okay.*
> —Michael Singer

Purpose, Layer-Caked

I believe that our lives are filled with purpose, just by the virtue of being here. If you're still breathing, your job isn't done. I'm not saying that it stops there, but from one breathing physical entity to another—you have a purpose to fulfill. Even a job to do.

As with most of my conceptual understanding of big questions that translates into something visual, a layer cake appears. So, too, with purpose: I see a couple of different layers. First, there is a base purpose, one that is the primary function in your being. Then, there are also more action-oriented purpose layers—one that has to do with your doing and another that has to do with a higher purpose. Being that we have come to the more spiritual part of the book, I need no raised eyebrows.

Ultimately, it is our base purpose that counts. The bottom layer. Without that, there are no other purposes to put on top of it. Like the essential bottom layer of a chocolate mud cake. What you put on this base layer, if anything, is really up to you. Without the base purpose, no other purpose has support. (Is your mind blown yet? Good.)

Base (BEING) Purpose: To be present

Your *being purpose* is to be present. By being "present" I mean to fully be yourself—to be alive, to be aware, to have fun, to feel joy. These are all authentic feelings that can only be experienced in the present moment. That's your base purpose.

Life, as we know it, can only be experienced in the present moment. That's why you're here: to be present. If you do only this, you are living on purpose. *Is that really enough?* Yes it is.

Most of us, myself included, are feeling an additional tug, a forward motion of sorts, which we experience as purpose as well. When you *are* your purpose (by being present), you can choose to apply that presence—the you that is uniquely you—to changing the world to something more beautiful than when you came here.

Additional (DOING) Purpose: To help make this world a better place

Your *doing purpose* is to help make this world a better place. By tapping into your power as a change-agent for good, you will see that the smallest and the biggest doings become meaningful.

Raising kind, honest and strong children is not a small favor to mankind. Spreading the kind of joy that emanates from presence is not a small gift to passengers as the train conductor punches holes, one by one, in their tickets. These are purposeful actions, as they come from presence.

We can go after the "bigger" things, too, in our *doing purpose*—starting an orphanage in a war-ridden country, inventing the internet, dividing the atom, saving the Arctic Sea, finding new cures for incurable diseases (just kidding! Since Mr. Polio, no one seems to aim for that one), exploring space, working to balance gender equality or racial biases, inventing the wheel, etc.

The importance of your *doing purpose* is not the size of your endeavor; it is the intention with which you approach it.

Additional (UNIVERSAL) Purpose: To fulfill your part of a higher mind

Your *universal purpose* is to fulfill your part of a higher mind. By being open to a higher mind, you are making yourself available to do your part of this higher purpose.

Call it higher mind, spiritual interconnectedness, universal consciousness, the will of God, or the will of a universal intelligence... there is a force that we can connect with through our souls. This is a force that most people have encountered, but few have defined. And how can we? Words will never be enough for the power of this magical realm.

Whatever we call it, it is through presence, our base purpose, that we can access this force that connects each and every soul in the universe. And, yes, I personally include people who have passed from this physical world since, if you ask me, our souls never die. This is the infinite part of our power. There is just too much evidence to confidently suggest that people who have passed on can still connect specifically and sometimes even physically with those of us who are still here. (I told you it was going to get weird. Good to know, then, that there are more friends around than the ones we can see!).

> *To understand the immeasurable,*
> *the mind must be extraordinarily quiet, still.*
> —Jiddu Krishnamurti

Life is always growing. A force is pulling us and growing us that has yet to be explained by scientists. No one has even been able to explain what makes our fingernails grow. Sure, there are explanations of what happens on a cellular and molecular level, but what makes that molecular level move and "want" stuff? The universe is always expanding, no thanks to us. We have the choice to grow with this universal expansion or not. As life expands and we don't, we are left feeling empty. And all the while these concepts and words are abstract at best—we still don't know where our thoughts come from. Our brains can't think thoughts. It is something we use to think thoughts, but thoughts are not created in our brains.

**As little as a brain surgeon has seen a thought,
a heart surgeon has seen a soul.
It doesn't mean that they don't exist.**

I know I'm treading deep waters with this higher power stuff, and I'm trying to navigate my language in a way that doesn't turn you off, while at the same time, I really want you to find your own relationship to what a higher force means to you and can do for you. Because it is real.

You see, when you can connect with this deep intelligence that connects us all, you will be one cool businessperson.

When you tap into the depths of yourself and, thereby, can tap into other people's awareness, you will embrace the full power of your intuition.

Man, the things you'll be able to do.

I can't wait to see it.

Just out of curiosity: When have you felt tugged or pulled in a direction that defies logic? How often do you meet people who you instantly feel as if you have known your whole life? How many ideas have you had "out of no-where"? When have you taken a leap of faith? When have you felt that there is no turning back? When have you been so inspired that you haven't even paid attention to the impossibility of the tasks that will get you there, only to realize in hindsight that all those impossible events synchronized to see your vision through? When have you felt presence of something beyond yourself that has helped you make a choice, take a stance, or avoid the car crash? Have you even been miraculously (illogically) saved? How many times have you uttered, "it just didn't make sense!"

Looking back at my own business life, I have far too many examples of making decisions and producing work when I haven't been present, let alone in tune with my intuition or forces beyond. In these moments, I have not had access to myself and have just gone about business as usual. Mindless routine. A huge liability. Really annoying (and sometimes detrimental) results. Boring.

What excites me is to look at the other examples, when I have been present, and beyond connecting with myself have been able to connect with other people and powers... when I have seen events orchestrated before me that have been nothing short of miraculous. In these moments, I have felt part of a whole and that I have been taking care of my part of what has been wanting to be created by a higher mind.

The Business of Magic

Luckily, I have a million and a half examples from my business life where my intuition, physical intelligence, heart intelligence, soul intelligence, and a higher creative intelligence (and who knows what other helpers), have come to my aid.

In business, I have often felt protected, as if someone/something heard my clear intentions and delivered opportunities that matched it or took away what did not match it. *No contract here, meet new client here, happen to become friends with highly influential person there, catch the detrimental paragraph there, stumble upon a website that will change my life there, change your tickets there.* The strange thing is, that it's in the flow of not thinking too much or trying to control the situations too much that these protective moments have unfolded. Something else takes over in the presence of letting go.

In the creative process, I have often felt as if things are pointed out to me. I have a question and through me, I connect to this energetic realm around me and Boom, there it is. One of my teams may, as an example, have been working on concepts and ideas for some time, and as I enter the room to help them out, I see the one connecting word, the one connecting concept, that is needed to land the client or satisfy the project. I'm not *that* smart. But I can see it. It's as if the answer is hanging in the room, and no one else has volunteered to be the vessel to bring it out. Another creative source is there.

Or, if I have needed a visual to represent a whole concept, I have opened the one page in the one magazine that I have felt drawn to, and there it is! One picture that captures the coming visual concept for something that will be in everyone's fridge in Sweden for years to come. That can take three weeks to find. Or ten seconds.

When I've needed a quote or a name idea, they have literally and metaphorically fallen into my lap—a book placed on my desk, a menu in my lap, a song that happens to play on the radio, a mention from someone on the phone, a posting on Facebook—or I've driven by them on a big sign. My hands seem to have their own intelligence. As I get out of their way (by not thinking too much), they have solved seemingly impossible construction challenges by feeling it out. This is not on a local barbershop level, mind you, but on a national and global branding level. I guess I'm honking my own horn here, but only to the benefit for anyone to see the big advantage of being open to receiving help beyond our intellect and even beyond our own personal intelligence. These feats may sound small, but they make a huge difference for our creative abilities and our work efficiency, even on (perhaps particularly on) a big business level.

Thinking that I have been the mastermind behind all these seeming business miracles and too good to be true coincidences that I have experienced in my career would be straight up obtuse. I'm not alone in this. We're not alone in this. Our companies are not alone in this.

> *The deeper intelligence behind the mind*
> *is continually writing the best possible script for our life.*
> —Michael Neill

All these highflying words are to say that we are all energy—everything is energy and that energy in itself is a power source. Beyond the field of power that belongs to our perceived domain, the energy field we call ours either merges with other energy that matches its own or finds a relation to everything and everyone else. Either way, all energy impacts all energy—your energy impacts me, my energy impacts you, and our energy impacts our community; our community's energy impacts the world; the world's energy impacts you. This is why collective thinking is so powerful.

Thoughts are energy and come together to form powerful alliances. The awareness, the pull and the direction of this collective power is influenced by everybody's thinking, not just the ones with the same thoughts. Can you feel this energy sea going on in the world all the time? Pulling and tugging, pushing and shoving.

Right here, in the midst of this invisible power (energy), we live our lives, conduct our business, and perhaps try to make a difference. We've got nothing on this all-encompassing power field if we don't start tuning in with openness and great awareness. We have no idea if there is a creator to all of this or not. No one has definite answers to if this universal intelligence has a will or an intention of its own.

What we do know is that any motion can create momentum. In other words, objects and thoughts alike, just by starting to move, can generate more movement, and when the movement continues on its own, momentum is created. That's why Einstein said that nothing happens until something moves.

This higher mind most likely moves by its own momentum while influenced by the energy that we keep feeding it. As such, it is fair to at least ask some questions about it. Because what if this higher mind consists of more than the sum of everybody's energy that emanates from our thinking? What if it encompasses a direction of love and growth? What if there is guidance and help with every single step and at every single junction in your life? What if all of this is an invitation to explore who you truly are? Is it worth it to be too cool for school to even try these possibly life-altering inner dialogs? It's not like you have anything to lose. And who knows, you may even find your real self in the process.

Let go of the idea that you're a body that's destined to die,
and instead seek an awareness of your immortal self.
—Dr. Wayne Dyer

What I love about mindfulness is that we practice curiosity and we practice compassion. Anything we practice happens on all levels of awareness: in the meeting with self, in the meeting with another person, and in the meeting with the world (group, company, neighborhood). In other words, the curiosity and compassion starts in *us* and unfolds into the world.

What would happen in your business endeavors if you decide to approach yourself and how the world works with a newfound curiosity?

After all my research and experiences, I can safely say that there is definitely a powerful creative source to tap into. It is so powerful because it encompasses us all and draws energy and awareness from us all and makes consciousness and power available to everyone.

It's not until we all pitch in with our own heightened awareness that we impact the consciousness level on which the world operates. No one's suffering is separate from your suffering. Your ego thinks it's immune to this, but really, if you have any desire to have a joyful life, you cannot park yourself in your ego. If you have any desire to experience this life, it will be done (and can only be done) in presence. There you are, then, connected to everyone else. Your joy will become other people's joy. Your joyous presence will heal other people's suffering.

Translated to business terms, this means that you can't reach satisfying success if people who work for you feel like shit. You can't enjoy your rewards if they are made from generating more suffering to others. We can't outrun this. We can't hide. Eventually, your kids will be robbed or refugees will wash up on your private beach.

It also means that when you tap into this field of presence, joy and connectedness, you will build businesses that elevate people's quality of life, that make life easier for people (which will include you because it will start in you), and that will be an inspiration to people who work for you.

Whatever makes you feel authentically good is what will give you the most powerful position with which to approach life.

If your beliefs (or non-beliefs) are based on superiority, inferiority or indifference, it's your signal to open up to a new relationship to how you can feel good.

Just because I believe in a higher power (energy) and often sense the force of it does not mean that I haven't had bad experiences in business or that every single deal I have entered has been fabulous. That's actually quite the laugh as many egg-in-my-face experiences flash through my mind. It simply means that I have observed and felt the difference *in me* that have *preceded* the good deals and the bad deals. In other words, the way I think, feel, and to the degree of which I have been in awareness, have determined the outcomes for me.

What most often happens when I have my inner business in order is that results emerge beyond my wildest imagination. The energy trick behind this is that *I don't ultimately mind if the result is bad*. If it is, it just is. I refuse to have the ups and downs of the stock market determine the ups and downs of my emotional wellbeing. If shit happens, I choose to see it for what it might be: a gift for growing. If someone sees me handle anything differently, please read aloud to me from my own book. It'll be annoying, but I will need it.

A few people I have talked to seem to reason that if God or any kind of higher force existed, there would be nothing but peace and joy in the world, and if that manifestation-shit worked, everybody would drive around in a Lamborghini. Looking around, it is evident that we are far from a peaceful planet, and few drive the car of their dreams. The conclusion is, therefore, that God doesn't exist or is a mean mother trucker. Besides, they will add, only weak people with a fragile psyche would need such nonsense comfort as an invisible friend. Either way, this invisible force crap makes no sense to them.

So, let's take a deep breath and start by dialing down the language here by skipping the God word. Even Pope Francis says, "in a way, the traditional notion of God is outdated." Amen. We are left with a universal intelligence—that pull, that energy field, that higher mind beyond the capacity of human beings. And I can't help but wonder: how can we be so sure that we are supposed to have a pain-free existence when we are here? Why would suffering in the world make us completely discount any ideas of miracles and universal love? Who said we are not here to learn and to grow? All learning and grow-ing is connected with some amount of pain, so why is that not okay?

In spite of popularly misunderstood New Age messaging, we don't manifest what we want; we manifest what we *are*. So, as per Dr. Robert Holden, "pre-pare yourself for miracles today. Be open to what is beyond your theory of what you deserve and how the universe works."

Here's the real gift of believing in a bigger purpose: you recognize that the pain comes with gifts of learning, so that you actually take the painful experi-ence as an opportunity to grow. Otherwise, we live our whole lives on Super Mario level 1, just because we are afraid of the pain of hopping to the next beam. In other words, you will go through the same painful experience over and over and over again. You don't grow. You're still in pain. You don't make a higher level. You're caught in a Super Mario nightmare.

> *People say walking on water is a miracle,*
> *but to me walking peacefully on earth is the real miracle.*
> —Thich Nhat Hanh

If we all grow and realize that peace starts within each and every one of us, we will create heaven on earth. This is how you are a representative, how everybody is a representative, of the universal mind (collective energy field), and that it's not until everybody takes responsibility for his or her part of find-ing peace within that we can create peace everywhere. You can blame God all you want, but until you understand that you, by being a piece of this One mind, is the one responsible for doing the work of this idea we call God.

The ego will never get this. This higher power crap takes away from his own separateness and power perception, so of course we are in for a lost cause there. If we live in our left hemisphere of the brain, we will most certainly want to pull out the evidence that if there is a higher power for good while bad things are happening, it simply doesn't make sense. Better to protect our-selves from all this bad stuff in the world, being that there is evidence that people are bad. Walls go up; energy is blocked.

If we can all, *por favor*, step a little further into our authentic sides, away from the ego… if we can all shift over to the loving side, away from the fear side… if we can all dare to trust the wisdom housed in the right sides of our brain, away from the non-present left brain… if we can all just let out the fart already, be ourselves and have some fun together, we're looking at a pretty great place here within short.

After all my observations, it is safe for me to say that my openness and willingness to invite a higher force, reached through a clear and calm inner business, has pretty much determined the outcome of my business endeavors.

What fascinates me tremendously is that it is in the flow of not thinking too much that all this magic happens. There is a logical explanation to this (phew!), as the left side of our brains prevents us from being present and creative if we let it take over. This becomes quite the challenge as our whole culture and most of our business life is designed to encourage the left part of the brain to do our work. We feel smart there with our snappy language and impressive references. Turns out though, using it too much is not that smart. When we use the left side of our brain, we see life as linear and think almost exclusively about the past or about the future. We nit-pick endless details from our memories and thoughts about the future—information that we want to put in little boxes and slap categorized labels on. Although this calculated intelligence absolutely benefits us at times (duh!), those of you paying attention have already discovered the big flaw: Using our left brain hemisphere prevents us from being present. We are either in the past or in the future. We cannot experience life in the past or in the future, and we sure can't be creative and connected to others, remember?

Love is the bridge between you and everything
—Rumi

So, as lofty as it sounds, it is by steering your activities over to the right side brain hemisphere—the expressive, the artistic, the joyous, the goal-less, the unmeasured, the present side—that you will get the turbo benefit of your brain. This is sooooo annoying for a businessperson to hear. It's easier for a logical mind to accept that the more you think, the sharper you become. It's also logical to think that if we all work overtime, if only a couple of hours a day, we'll get a lot more work done. But it's simply not true, according to research and reality. Results like these don't match logical sense. Darn!

I have been under countless desperate deadlines to come up with strategies and ideas and visuals and concepts... all of which had to happen yesterday. I know what it feels like to be pressured in business, to have big financial worries with many people impacted; how it feels to be convinced that everything will fall apart if I don't nail this, if I don't work harder, if I don't deliver. It's inner hell and I'm sure you know what I'm talking about.

It took me a few years to figure out a couple of important pointers on the matter. You see, the whole working harder, pushing harder, and pressuring my team harder turned out to be counter-productive. Who knew? We're back to the human experience of being here.

Here's my logic:

- If I allow myself to have fun and express myself creatively, I am training my right side of the brain to come to my rescue in any other situation. Don't discount having fun and doing things you love as fruitless nonsense. As your capacity for right brain activity grows, so does your ability to handle stress, worry and anger.
- If I approach business situations with stress, worry or anger, I am effectively cutting myself off from any help that is willing to step in, be it help from within myself, from other people, or from whatever these invisible forces are. Anger really does block the way for anyone or anything willing to help you. Being pissed off with work-related matters does not give you a free pass.
- Tapping into a beneficial part of the collective energy does not work when you doubt your own connection to greatness. It does not work if you are afraid to miss out on what other people are doing, stealing focus from your own task at hand.

- Above all, it is in the relaxation of knowing that whatever happens, you can choose not to mind. Then there will be magic in your approach.

Love + Magic = Logic

When you feel ready to live in an awareness-proximity to a bigger energy field, when you are willing to give up some of your perceived control, get in to the flow of things and access help from a bigger realm, there are some things you can do in your approach.

For one, know that your intuition responds to questions. You can always take a moment with yourself and ask some questions to which you are honestly ready to hear the answers. Perhaps you have a business situation where you are about to hire someone. *Is this a good hire?* you ask yourself. (Since you have connected with yourself, your intuition will know what you mean/feel by "good", because you are there already). You may continue: *Will this person be an uplifting force for my team?* (Sit with it). Is this person resilient in times of pressure?

Or perhaps you have other business related matters to discuss with yourself and all that is connected to you: *Will this business deal take me towards my vision of [insert vision here]? Can I trust this consultant to deliver on time? Am I making the right decision for the company to fire this person now?*

As you meet yourself in silence and ask yourself questions, stay open to how you hear the answers. With yes or no questions, stay open to how you hear the yes or the no; is it a voice, is it a "knowing" or does it affect your breathing in a certain way? Other types of answers may come to you as you start moving about in the world, where answers, directly relating to your question, appear. It really can be that simple and I look forward to hearing how you have connected with your intuition and what signs, symbols and communication you have developed. It takes a little testing, so have fun while you're doing it.

Congruency with the creative Source of the universe
in your own Divine imagination makes what you wish for
not only probable but dead-on inevitable.
—Dr. Wayne Dyer

As I am rounding off this s-word section of the book, I just have to say that I don't have any agenda whatsoever to make you a believer. I work with the inner business of business and want to share all tools that have placed both me and my team on a higher level in business. This energy business just happens to be one of them. When I trust a higher power, it reminds me that I am "small" enough to not see the bigger picture all the time. I don't have all the answers. Coining yourself as "small" is bound to rub some people the wrong way, especially amongst us business women who have fought hard to see ourselves as big and have others respect us as powerful in our own right. So, to put it in other words; as grand as I am, there is an infinite power still that I can tap into. How about that for empowering?

Now, for those of you who skimmed through this spirituality stuff, you can put your listening ears back on as we now welcome you back.

Mindfulness Attitude: Letting Go

Leaders are usually compelled to control—a trait that can sink even the best of us. The old paradigm of conducting business with an iron fist is not only old, it is directly damaging for business development and your mental health. As you refuse to let go, you hold on to too many things that don't serve you, and you lose your position of power. As you hold on, your whole system is tense; you close yourself off intellectually, emotionally and physically. That is the opposite of what we need in a powerful leader.

If you are not willing to let go of control, you won't be able to expand, neither as a person nor as a business. In this unwillingness, you negate the fact that it takes more than you and the limits of your mind to make something grow. You want to control everything, which is impossible. That's very stressful.

> *Power, at its core, is letting go of resistance.*
> —Abraham

Add to that the dire need for so many companies to elevate their creative senses, their innovation capacity, and the speed with which they operate and make decisions. You will get none of these for the price of control. Creativity happens in the letting go of the calculated. Innovation happens in the letting go of what we hold true. Efficiency happens in the letting go of limiting our doing to intellectual pursuits. Anything authentic happens in the letting go of our ego.

No one is happy when they contract their whole beings in order to control everything; yet, it is unbelievably difficult for many of us to let go. *What if I don't make sure everything is working? The company will fall apart! I have to be this controlling! I have to be everywhere! All the time!*

Everybody else knows that the company will not fall apart in your absence, but that's how it actually feels for the person who has diluted his mind into thinking that he is in complete control of everything. Needless to say, nothing should be dealt with in isolation. If you have, indeed, hired complete idiots in an unsafe work environment and given them no information on what to do whatsoever, then, of course, you better go control things. Seriously! Stop reading and go fix it. Somebody call someone!

Under more normal circumstances, however, where we have a somewhat healthy team and a good vision for what we are actually doing, some people still have the most difficult time letting go. How about you?

I don't want you now berating yourself for being controlling. We are just observing without judging.

Mindfulness is a useful tool because it leaves it to you to explore the workings of you. So be gentle with yourself when you examine what, in you, could contribute to your urge to control and your unwillingness to let go. You know now that it is in your better interest, in the real world, to do so.

The beauty of letting go is that it leaves room to be happily surprised. My bet is that in your years of "being in control," not everything has turned out the way you planned, yes? And I bet that some things—out of your control—turned out to be worse for you, and that some things turned out better. Yes again?

Knowing what feels good to you is one of your greatest sources of power. But feeling good is not easy when you hold on to your set beliefs about how things should be done, your set idea of how things should turn out, and your stubborn thoughts on who should do what. Can you pass by that resistance and feel what feels good for you? Not just as a sensation; I mean good in the depths of you—the kind of good that has longevity to it, perhaps even a sniff of eternity. Sit with that feeling. What if you could feel these things most of the time? What if your experience of the atmosphere is yours to determine? Remember, life happens *for* you. What if you felt great, everybody working with you felt great, and the company felt great? Would you be prepared to let go of what no longer serves you *before* that can happen?

Mindfulness Attitude: Trust

As I have mentioned before, of all the attitudes in mindfulness, *trust* is a word that echoes throughout many management tricks and leadership success lists out there. And no wonder—if people don't trust you, you will have a hard time making powerful changes for your company.

In these other leadership contexts, trust is often spoken of as *displaying of trust*: consistency, credibility and competence. Trust is a feeling to instill in other people about you. Make people feel that they can trust you to make the right choices—not mess up—and be transparent enough and meet the bottom line. Trust as a means to an end.

In a mindfulness context, trust does not start with other people. In a mindful business way, trust is not about exuding an aura of trust to your employees. Here, trust is found in the relationship to yourself and how you see the world.

Trusting yourself doesn't have to do with trusting your performance. It goes deeper than that. It has to do with you starting to trust that you are enough—that you bring value to the world just by being you and by expressing who you really are. If you are really stressed out about your business performance right now and wonder what the point of this slow-moving trust stuff is, bear with me. Because when you learn to trust your sense of you—that you have the ability to distinguish valuable core-based insights from fruitless ego-based knee-jerk reactions—it will serve you well. Particularly in business.

In relation to other people, trust is the opposite of trying to command or control. In fact, trying to control others is a deep disservice to yourself as you prove to yourself that you trust neither life nor yourself. With real trust, there is willingness and a mutual bond; there is no need for control. Trust is a choice, available for anyone. Sometimes, it is earned, proved or rewarded, but that's not necessary. If I choose to trust you, that's my choice.

The ability and choice to trust is your own true power, whereas command and control is a self-induced or company-appointed dominance. You may have deservedly reached an executive position of power in your company, or you may not have. That aside, your true power—that which stands independent of corporate rules and company pecking orders—is an interdependent system between your true self and others. Again, Mr. Ego has no room here since he would be the first one to waive the corporate pecking order card. You really have no use for him as you venture to connect with a deeper power within you. The more you can leave ego outside this structure, the more powerful you will be.

What is important to recognize is that there is no way to short-circuit trust. Trust will always be a genuine choice, and it always has to start in you. First, you come to a place of trusting yourself—trusting that you know who you are and are devoted to a true sense of yourself. Then, you'll have gained the foundation of extending that trust to other people. As you grow in your trust, it will extend to an ability of trusting and be trusted by your company, your community, and the world. As you trust yourself, you will also open up for other people to trust you.

Because now they actually can.

You cannot give what you don't have.

There are few things that will help you in business and life as much as trusting that life ultimately wants you well. If you dare to trust that life is really happening *for* you and not *to* you, life will turn sweet pretty quickly. Not to mention how many opportunities you suddenly will be open to seeing. In my experience and observation, the real mind-shift—that opens up our minds to be trained to even bigger capacity—includes trusting a higher form of yourself.

Like we have explored before and that I'm sure you have felt many times, there is something inside you that just *knows*... there is something in you that can observe you... something that is removed from your life's drama, like a wise influence. It's as if this sense is connected to everything and everybody else. How else could we know? This intelligence orchestrates seemingly impossible events and makes unknown forces come to your aid. How else could it all happen?

Without a shred of religious connotation, I think we all (no matter what we call it) have felt moments when we just know there are larger powers at play, forces we cannot grasp, and an unexplainable strength that keeps us going. There is something in this connectedness that makes us feel that everything will be okay. In fact, that everything *is* okay, even during hard times. At least, that is a choice.

When you develop a trust to this bigger force, bigger things will start to happen. And as we have already discussed in the recent perhaps-a-tad-too-spiritual-for-everyone part of the book, at closer examination, it makes perfect sense: The more you summon the forces that are connected with everything and everyone else, the bigger things can be orchestrated.

A good sound bite for any situation that makes you want to run for cover under the wings of ego, self-doubt or self-pity is: *"All is well."* That is a trusting choice available for you, should you be interested in summoning your powers to seeing things turn around.

The Briefing on POWER

- **Your power is as big as the enormity of your natural powers minus all the power-draining mental activities you allow in your life. For instance, the garbage pile of thought clutter you have centrifuging around there in your mind, or any other type of resistance you feel yourself up against.**

- **Here's how you are power:**
    - **You are energy (everything is energy and energy is power).**

- You are authority (you make all your decisions, including letting other people control you).
- You are light (the creative power that can outshine any darkness).
- You are a change-agent for good (as your power to act is one for a better world).

- You are actually powerful beyond belief. It's up to you if you use your power as a change-agent for good or as a control factor for gain.

- The door to your power opens inwards. Stop pushing.

- Figure out what drains your power. Does believing that you are victim, negative self-talk, trying to control other people or hanging out with other power suckers strike a chord?

- Most of our feelings are produced by our thoughts. So here's the happiness recipe: We can choose what we think.

- True power = Listening + Alignment + Motion
  - Listening = the deep listening that is beyond mind-made concepts.
  - Alignment = Awareness + Intention + Trust.
  - Motion = action that comes from listening and alignment.

- Learn how to differentiate between the intention that comes from your ego and the intention that comes from your true you. The latter is you real power force. Your ego will never ever be happy with you. Ever. So there's no real power to get from there.

- Sometimes it's necessary to say No on the outside. But you will always be powerful if you say Yes on the inside. You don't have to agree with what is happening, but if you don't accept it (say yes on the inside) you will spend your time and power arguing over what has already happened and that which cannot be undone. Say yes, save the energy, and solve the problem with a clear, uninterrupted mind.

- Maturity = Awareness + Experience

- Here's your purpose:
    o Your BEING purpose is to be present. That's it.
    o Your DOING purpose is to help make this world a better place. In the small and in the big.
    o Your UNIVERSAL purpose is to fulfill your part of a higher mind. Oh yeah. And if you haven't read the whole chapter (Skimmer!) you don't get to protest.

- Here's the real gift of believing in a bigger purpose: you recognize that pain comes with gifts of learning, so that you actually take the painful experiences as opportunities to grow. Then you don't need to have more pain sent your way for that lesson, thank you very much!

- If you completely want to diminish yourself and sabotage the glorious reason why you are here, you totally have to believe that you are a victim, you definitely always should blame everyone for anything gone the slightest wrong (including yourself) and you should take no responsibility for how you impact the world. That should do it.

- Or, you can accept your powerful awesomeness and start changing the world to someone through-and-through beautiful. Starting with yourself.

POWER – Mind-Training Exercise

It is time for you to really examine what drains your power. As we have already established, in the core of our beings we are powerful beyond measure and we can change the world to something much more beautiful than it was when we first graced it with our presence. So let's look at some of the things that bog you down, that suck your power—and make changes for a more powerful you. Here are some examples, some that we have explored more in-depth and others that you may recognize from your own life.

1. Believing that you are a victim
2. Getting stuck in a wheel of negative emotions
3. Thinking that your power comes from the outside
4. Negative self-talk
5. Trying to control other people
6. Competing with others (on an ego-level)
7. Engaging in judgmental speculation
8. Hanging out with other power suckers
9. Thinking that reality should be different than it is
10. Feeling chronically/often-times stressed

Reflect on which power drainers strike a cord with you. Can you let go of any of them? Take note of your thought-process and resistance. Also add your own personal power drainers.

Notes:

POWER – Meditation Practice

Walking Meditation: 5-15 minutes

Stand up straight in a room where you have enough space in front of you to walk a few steps, at the least. The longer the better. Relax your arms and hands along the sides of your body. Feel your body standing tall and straight, without being strained or stiff. You are relaxed and alert. You are feeling the big presence of your body. There it is, taking up space. There you are, with your body. Standing. And being breathed. You can put your gaze down to the floor, to limit the visual impressions while still seeing where you are about to walk.

Notice how your body reacts as it knows that you are about to take a step. Is it preparing for the movement? Is it tensing up, already on its way? Is it contracted as the mind wants to get on with the movement already? Feel how the soles of your feet are meeting the floor. Feel your weight on the exact surfaces that meet the floor. Now, very, very slowly, start taking a first step forward. It will be a small step and it will be very slow. You will have time to notice every movement; your different muscles that are involved in getting the one foot off the ground; the shift in body balance that is required to lift the one foot without tipping over that way. You are completely focused on moving one foot in the trajectory of one step. As your foot touches the floor again, this time a little bit in front of you, you will shift your body weight forward, as you prepare to take your next step with your other foot. You are feeling the first foot's meeting with the floor as you are sensing the other foot starting to get relieved from your total body weight. It starts to lift as well, and you are there, experiencing the movement. You can feel your body breathing as you slowly take your second step. Your belly is expanding with your breath, and perhaps you can feel your clothes tugging a little around the waist. You observe how your arms and shoulders feel as you are continuing your forward motion, transitioning from your second to your third step. As per Thich Nhat Hanh, you can continue to walk as if your feet kiss the ground. You have no physical destination to reach, other than if you do run out of floor space, you slowly turn around and walk back. You can walk the same track back and forth many times as you practice presence and bodily awareness in a walking meditation.

I suggest starting with a few minutes, perhaps five. And as you get more used to being present and focused, you can add on more time.

Meditation Quick Fix: 2 minutes

I urge all my students to walk one of the blocks to work in a walking meditation. Not only will you get a few minutes of mindfulness meditation in to your schedule without any extra effort, you will also practice not caring what people think of you!

Here's how you do it: Choose a distance in your walking route, one block is great, and slowly walk in complete awareness of your bodily movement as you are walking. You may not be walking as slowly as you do when you are doing a walking meditation at home or in a meditation group, but you will be walking slowly enough to feel your body moving on the streets. Start by connecting with your feet inside your shoes, really feel your feet. Put your gaze down somewhat and start your slow, mindful walk. Please make sure to be safe, both from cars, bikes and other people. Start with two minutes and notice how you are more connected to the glorious you -- beneficial for whatever you are facing next.

Are You Joking?

I'd like you to think back to earlier, when I shared that as a CEO, I had a New Business experiment running where I had one pool of prospects I chased "as per usual," and another pool I intently and intensely "only" focused on. A cold-calling versus manifestation experiment, one could say.

Well, I ran this experiment for quite some time, compared the results and made note of how I felt and what actually worked. In short: I got to know myself in relation to the power of my attention, the pull of what I find attractive (on more levels that just physical), as did I in relation to business as a collective. And, more specifically, to the parts, people and products that make up what we refer to as business. What really happened was that I got to truly experience the mechanics of my business intuition.

Since I bought my first tube of lip-gloss, I've had a love for drug stores. Anything from nail polish to nutrition has intrigued me, so, no wonder, as the head of a design agency, there were several brands in the drugstore that I really, really wanted to work with. Now, back then in Sweden, there was just one drugstore chain that was state-owned. It has since been released to some different players, but that's irrelevant to the story.

At the time I'm speaking of, my agency already had a couple of clients with brands sold in the drugstore. As per my usual New Business Prospects routine, I was browsing the drugstore, looking for more products in the space. I noticed a brand I wasn't familiar with and it really stood out in my mind. It was just a logotype on the back of a package, but somehow, it spoke to me. This was my way of being open to intuitive "hits" when I was out and about. Since the consumer goods space was my area of expertise and interest, this openness to an "anomaly experience" was especially valuable as I browsed the aisles at different stores for new prospects. (And no, there is probably very little coincidence that my agency's roster of clients included those of chocolate, candy, ice cream, baby products, organic produce and other lust products.)

I still don't know what made this particular company stand out and demand my attention, and, luckily, I had given up the habit of questioning these things. So I decided to look it up.

As I quickly researched the company's website, I came across a picture of a marketing manager in Norway. Among all the faces there, her face interested me; she looked kind and open. So I called the company, asked for her and she picked up the phone! (Boy, one thing I miss in the US is the Scandinavian lack of gatekeepers!).

We spoke then and there, and I sent her a sample portfolio during our call. She told me she loved what she saw, that she got a good vibe from me (!) and that it was funny I should call. "Our Director of Marketing is looking at doing a redesign before the launch of one of our brands. Let me give you his cell phone number." (How about that for Scandinavian ways...)

I don't like making sales calls, but this was an easy one to make. Besides, when you're a CEO responsible for feeding 30 people, you do a lot of things you don't necessarily like doing. I called him up, introduced myself, and do you know what he said? "Are you joking?"

It was so synchronistic that he thought I was pulling a prank. He said, "I am literally in a cab right now, on my way from an agency that just presented a design I need to put into production, and it sucks. I really don't want this design, but have no other options."

So of course I invited him to meet with us.

He came to our office, I did a brief portfolio presentation and he seemed to like what he heard and saw. I told him, "I know you spent a lot of money on an agency that hasn't delivered. I'm going to give you this opportunity. You pay us close to nothing until our first design presentation, if you don't like it, we will not charge you. If you do like it, we'll go ahead with the project and you pay us our full fee."

Cut to ten days later, we presented our designs to him, he loved it and we were hired.

Within the first year of our design reaching the drug store shelves, this fluoride rinse brand owned a third of the market in Sweden. It was the fourth highest over-the-counter brand (not including pain relievers) in Sweden. At the time of this writing, almost ten years later, they still have a third of the market and they were a valuable client for the agency for many years.

All this was allowed to unfold because I didn't doubt my intuitive "hit" in the drug store that day, and because I acted on the impulses I felt from the photo of a warm, friendly woman. I listened to that which spoke to me, and that inspired me to make a fortuitous call.

Don't underestimate what happens in business when you dare to live in an inspired state of not constantly second-guessing yourself.

When you train your mind to be clear, you discover a state of flow within yourself. And with others. And with other things. It's all about energy, remember? So get your ducks in a row with talented people, a deep interest in learning things and jump on the flow of good stuff. Trust yourself.

A Light on Spark

I could call this section "inspirational-state-of-flow-and-connection-to-many-things," but I've chosen to call it "spark." (It has a nicer ring to it, doesn't it?)

Spark is the final step on our journey from feeling stuck to experiencing freedom. Learning is never linear and neither is this trip. For every circular motion you make through the modules of this program—BEING, FOCUS and POWER—you reach a kind of maturity and lightness necessary for acquiring real SPARK.

Spark is filling yourself up with more of the true you so that you have even more of you to express. You become more than just a drop in the ocean as you realize that you are the ocean.

Spark is a state that holds one of the most important reasons to why we are here; our ability to express ourselves—what is uniquely you and what is uniquely me. When we are sparked to express ourselves, we are connecting with collective intelligence through the depths of ourselves. Spark is truly a state of inspiration.

To be inspired means to live *in-spirit*. This is a place that knows no limits to creativity, no boundaries between anything and it certainly holds no glass ceiling above you. Your joy for self-expression, as it comes from the true depths of you and not the ego space of proving, getting, wanting, is the kind of joy that the world can't get enough of.

When you cultivate spark, the world can't get enough of you.

When you inspire others, you strike a chord in others to live in-spirit. You are in a state of spark as you are sharing your spirit and letting the creative light shine through you. Your spark is what lights your passion. Your spark can inspire other people to turn on their lights. Your spark can set the world on fire.

So the question is; are you extroverted, beautiful, successful and wealthy? Congratulations, then you will have what the average-looking Joe will never have: Spark! Oh you lucky duck.

Of course I'm joking.

Funny though, that this is how many of us ordinary people walk around. Thinking that living in a charged state of feeling and having a life-affirming spark is reserved for the already successful people of the world.

If this is what you believe—that "spark" is reserved for the uber-successful—you are actually making a choice *not* to be ignited on the inside as you take on your days. Your misinformed beliefs about spark and creative flow make you live your life as if you've already given up.

And this is not only sad, but it is all too common.

Many of us are too soaked in self-doubt or self-pity to fire up our own spark. The limitations we put on ourselves (and allow others to put on us) are quite mind-boggling. Why on earth would we put a lid on our deepest longing – to have our spirit express itself? What happened along the way? Between our pathology and lack of value, we mosey around from one must-do on our list to another. "*Okay, okay, I'll do it* [the "it" being life]. *Quit twisting my arm.*" Or perhaps you sport the hysterical version of the same attitude, constantly feeling chased to complete an overwhelming string of tasks every day, feeling panicked and screaming bloody murder at every turn. Either way, we live as if someone else were dictating the state of our lives. As if our real life will roll around some other day. As if living a life of inspiration is something reserved for other people. And don't even get me started on how far fetched it would be to imagine living a life devoted to inspiring others.

Or could it be that we're simply misinformed? Perhaps we are not in touch with ourselves enough to even fathom living in spirit, an inspired life. In spark.

But of course, this is why I'm speaking to you from the pages of this book.

If we shed some much-needed light on the question of Spark, we'll all be inspired to start firing ourselves up. Yes, even you. Yes, even your partner. Yes, even your co-worker and your mother. But that'll be up to them. So let's get started by addressing some common misconceptions.

First of all, you must understand that an inner spark can express itself in a number of different ways. Sometimes it glimmers in the calm air of confidence. Sometimes it shines warmly in loving actions. Other times, spark is an explosion of possibilities, or a passionate fire storming the world.

To spark, it does not matter if you are an extrovert, an introvert or any other type of vert. Whichever disposition or temperament spark takes on, its source is always rooted in a meaningful passion for making a difference.

Spark is not charm.

Spark is not charisma.

Spark goes way beyond that.

Spark is fueled by love.

**Anyone who chooses to trade self-pity and ego
for a passionately meaningful life will feel spark.
This is how it's available to anybody at any time.**

Richard Branson has been quoted as saying, "*If you aren't making a difference in people's lives, you shouldn't be in business, it's that simple.*" This extraordinarily successful man and unconventional leader keeps coming back to a core of passionate contribution and joyous responsibility. His whole business empire is built on his inspired idea that life can be fueled with more fun for more people. He has built companies as diverse as airlines and record labels with the same brand name and the one big umbrella theme of entertainment. His example of leadership way outside the rulebook has inspired hundreds of thousands of other leaders. A recent example is that he apparently has started letting his employees work without being measured in time, just in results. In other words, his employees can show up when they feel like it, as long as they get their tasks done. I don't even fully support this unconventional idea, and still find it very inspiring!

In my book, (so to speak) Richard Branson is the perfect example of an inspiring leader because he exudes who he truly is while encouraging those around him to express who they truly are. Just look at him! That's a guy who lives in-spirit. And yes, he's gotten monetarily rich in the process. But make no mistake: The horse is spirit, the riches is the cart.

We all know what spark feels like. At least I hope so. It's that vibrancy of feeling alive that just makes everything exciting – like we're part of something big and wonderful, and we feel like the chosen vessels for this greatness. Filled with spark, there seems to be no end to the light we can shine on others and the positive effect we have on people around us. When we go on a stage and feel our spark, the audience is mesmerized and we can say nothing wrong. When we are in strategic work meetings and feel it, the right solutions just flow out of us. When we feel it as we meet with our co-workers, we can sense how we inspire them to do their best. And man, when it's with us as we enter a negotiation, we just know how to nail it. These are the rewards in connecting with that state, with spark.

In business, choosing spark is the smart thing to do. We feel great, we feel "on purpose", we feel alive, we feel connected and, as if the enjoyment of the process wasn't enough, we also see great results. Yet, few of us choose to live in spark.

> **We're treating our spark as if it's fine-china.**
> **Either we don't have it, we don't use it,**
> **or we only bring it out on special occasions.**

Perhaps we think that spark chooses us, giving no thought to the fact that it might even be *possible* to choose it for ourselves.

You may think that this "it" quality is something a few people are born with and, if you weren't, then, tough luck. If that is part of your belief system, try to turn your thinking around to welcoming the idea that anyone can cultivate spark. That it is, in fact, not just reserved for a fortunate few, or the beautiful ones, or the extroverted ones.

Everybody has love and light that can shine through and inspire the world.

> *There's a crack in everything.*
> *That's how the light comes in.*
> —Leonard Cohen

Speaking as a juggling businesswoman and a single parent of a young child in a hustling big city, I know for sure that we are capable of choosing spark in seemingly impossible situations. And our spark really doesn't have to spew out as fireworks around the clock. Talk about exhausting!

I personally love to think of our spark as an inner glow that gets cultivated when we are still, contemplating, enjoying silence and solitude. This inner glow is very potent and inspires people even through brief encounters. That's at least what my new beautician sincerely meant as I was lying on her table, spread eagle for a Brazilian, when out of nowhere she asked me if I was an inspirational speaker. She knew nothing of me, except, ehm, perhaps more than most in some detailed matters, but picked up an inspired feeling, just from our encounter. When I said "yes" she repeatedly exclaimed, "I *knew* it!" as she was getting my "other" inner business in order.

Spreading light on mundane situations will impact people's lives for the better. Now, let's get that Brazilian wax scene out of our heads please. (The things I'll do to inspire spark!)

When in spark, you are doing nothing but showing up in presence. The presence you exude as you check in at the airport can shift the energy around you from hysterical and hostile to calm and cooperative. The coworkers who had a terrible morning feel better just with your sincere hello. The tired waitress finds a spring in her step from your friendly demeanor.

You access spark through your being, not from a calculated doing. In other words, your doing comes from the fact that you *are* the light you are spreading, and anything you do becomes an action of light. Get the order straight here, because if you are not sensing and living in the core of your light first, you are walking around as an open invitation to Mr. Ego. Any doing with measurable results and calculated outcomes will make this a competition for Mr. Ego. We are on the subject of inspiration and he's old news! Mr. Ego has no place in spark.

Remember that your light is enough.

And when we need the shining beacon of a lighthouse, that's when we really set that spark on fire!

Cultivating Spark

Behold! There are some sure-fire ways to cultivate spark. One thing we can't do, however, is to fake our way to spark—neither romantically nor otherwise.

What do I mean by that? Well, let's say you desire the same kind of spark as someone in your life who seems to have "it". Perhaps you're picturing a charismatic businessman working the tradeshow floor. He oozes confidence as he creates connections and leaves a trail of smiles behind him as he swaggers through the room. Everyone pockets his business card with care.

If you start mimicking his every step and repeating his lines—without having your own spark cultivated—you would not come close to having the same effect. You might even suppress your own spark.

People can *feel* the difference between someone who has cultivated real spark (who has "it") and someone who is trying too hard (who's faking it). Some of us have even tried to fall in love with someone who is "so right" for us, only to realize that, as opposed to red hair or orgasms, romantic spark cannot be faked.

More importantly, you can feel the difference between what is real in you and what is not. It may be more of an uncomfortable hum and a funky feeling at first. But the more you get in touch with yourself, the more you can define what is real so you can get clearer on what will get your inner fire stoked. Then you can turn the nagging feeling of what doesn't feel right into a clearer understanding of what constitutes your own personal truth.

Keys To Spark – How To Get "It"

In order to learn how to get "it", you will have to wade through some deep fundamental questions of life. Easy peasy. These questions, I consider the keys to spark. When you figure out who you are and why you're here, add in some curiosity, imagination and kindness? Well. The sky is the limit. Here are the keys (ie: How to get "it"):

- Connect with and accept yourself (*Who Am I?*)
- Be passionate about making a meaningful difference (*Why am I here?*)
- Get on the imagination train (*How Am I a Creator?*)
- Always practice kindness (*What's My Ticket?*)

Who Am I?

And here we are. Back to the most basic, but always relevant question: Who am I? The more times you ask yourself this question, the more informative your answer will be. BEING is the basis of this entire mind-training program, and we really have to know our being before taking any valuable steps as a leader. As you know by now, the answer to your question will not just be intellectual. It will not just be descriptive. When you have asked yourself *Who am I? Who am I really? Who am I even beyond that? Who am I in the essence of that which is beyond who I thought I was?* The answer will not be; I am an Accountant.

Now that you have learned how to move beyond the fruitless answers of the ego, take a moment and reflect on who you really are, if you haven't done so already. Perhaps you may wish to start by noticing your reactions to the question itself. What are the judgments that come up?

We have a couple of different layers of judgments to explore here, as we first need to look at what you are thinking about the exercise itself. *Who needs to ask such a freakin' stupid question in the first place? I'm an Accountant for Pete's sake!*

You may even go off on an anger rant, like Adam Sandler's character in the movie Anger Management. The group therapist leader, brilliantly portrayed by Jack Nicholson, asks this very question as Sander's character joins the group. "Who are you?" After a couple of unsuccessful attempts of answering the question with "Well, I'm an Executive Assistant…" and "I'm a pretty good guy, I play tennis…" he continues to get the instruction to tell the group who he is, not what he does or what hobbies he has. Clearly not digging the depth of the question, he even asks the group for an example of what a good answer would be. After some mocking laughs from the group and yet another comment that they are not interested in knowing his personality, just who he is, he finally snaps in anger. That is candy for an anger management group therapy leader, but perhaps not so sweet for you.

Another judgment to look out for when you ask yourself such a profound question is that of your own process. As you judge yourself, you effectively close yourself off from You—the opposite of what we want when we want to connect with who we really are.

I can't tell you who you are. This is your enriching and elevating process. What I can do though, is give you some pointers to start your dialog. I have cherry-picked a list of life-pointers from a flora of different wise people. If they resonate with you, bring them in to your contemplation on the awe-inspiring subject of You. Perhaps you will feel inspired or encouraged, perhaps one of them gives you a little aha-moment of your idea of life, that it says something about you that you haven't put in to words yet, or perhaps they are all valuable as different angles of your you-exploration. If not, skip them, just don't judge them. Perhaps you even want to save some for later.

Here they are:

- To be yourself in a world that is constantly trying to make you something else, is the greatest accomplishment. —Ralph Waldo Emerson

- I've learned that people will forget what you said, people will forget what you did, but people will never forget how you made them feel. —Maya Angelou

- I exist as I am, that is enough. —Walt Whitman

- To realize who you are not, that is freedom —Byron Katie

- That it will never come again is what makes life so sweet. —Emily Dickinson

- A man who lives fully is prepared to die at any time. —Mark Twain

- Peace is not merely a distant goal that we seek, but a means by which we arrive at that goal. —Martin Luther King, Jr.

- Be the change you want to see in the world. —Mahatma Gandhi

- It'll all be okay in the end. If it's not okay, it's not the end. —John Lennon

- Darkness cannot drive out darkness; only light can do that. Hate cannot drive out hate; only love can do that. —Martin Luther King, Jr.

- Our prime purpose in this life is to help others and if you can't help them, at least don't hurt them. —His Holiness Dalai Lama

- Spread love wherever you go. Let no one ever come to you without leaving happier. —Mother Teresa

- When you think everything is someone else's fault, you will suffer a lot. When you realize that everything springs only from yourself, you will learn both peace and joy. —His Holiness Dalai Lama

- I believe in pink. I believe that laughing is the best calorie burner. I believe in kissing, kissing a lot. I believe in being strong when everything seems to be going wrong. I believe that happy girls are the prettiest girls. I believe that tomorrow is another day and I believe in miracles. —Audrey Hepburn

- To see a world in a grain of sand and heaven in a wild flower. Hold infinity in the palms of your hand and eternity in an hour. —William Blake

Here's what I came to think of about myself when I read these life pointers:

Now take your moment with your life-companion of a question: *"Who am I?"* before we move on to this companion's sister; another profound question.

Why Am I here?

If you haven't already, you will do well by finding out what your bigger reason is to be here—what on earth you're doing on earth. Here, you will find your passion for making a difference. If you don't know what makes you spring out of bed in the morning, it's hard to make that inspired choice.

I'm sure that on some level, you want to make a difference in the world. So, what is that? Big picture? Can you see it and feel it?

When you can connect with that sense of meaningful contribution that can make a difference in the world, really note that feeling. Relish in it. That's a spark. Whatever senses you connect with it (emotion, smell, visual), savor it for a while. That is the sensory North Star of your spark that you will focus on as you start taking steps in that very direction. You don't even need to have all the answers and know what every step is about; you stick with the feeling of your North Star—that's your job, and that's what will get you there.

In this life we cannot do great things.
We can only do small things with great love.
—Mother Teresa

It will always be on the *inside* of us that we will find our spark. Even if our mission includes outside definitions, it is an inside job to find the spark that will make you complete your mission. There is an internal reason as to why your external vision shows up. Tune in with that. Your spark can only be lit in your own presence.

We have to be mindful of the order of things here. In order for us to align with all the available solutions for our vision, we need to first align with ourselves and light our own spark. It is only when we have connected with our inner spark that we will make connecting with something outside ourselves possible. This is where I personally think that mindfulness meditation is such a brilliant practice.

With mindfulness meditation techniques, we are practicing presence and inner connection in our everyday lives. There are so many stresses and distractions that will side-track us from our true missions. As we move around life in our getting-going-doing-wanting-modes (never in the now), mindfulness practice reminds us how to live life without losing our connection with our presence. Anything else in life that you want to get good at, you practice. Be it learning a new language, playing an instrument or running the marathon, you need to practice. And we accept that. Why is it so hard for most of us to accept that we need to practice awareness and focus? It's not strange.

The seemingly "too simple" exercises of practicing being fully present, focusing on our breathing and our bodies all of a sudden seem to make sense, no?

Spark Through Meditation

Going even further in our meditation reason-to-be, we can look at meditation as it relates to spark and connection. Here are some inspiring examples of how a meditation practice may guide us:

- ***By being aware of our own breathing, we can breathe with others.*** When you tune in to another person's breathing, while feeling your own, it makes you aware of which state that person is in, and how you can best connect with the person. Can you imagine having the ability to avoid putting people off, to be sensitive to their mental and emotional space, and to understand how to best make your voice heard?

- ***By creating a gap between your true self and your ego-doings, you can observe both yourself and others with some distance.*** As you learn how to watch yourself from a little distance, you are effectively shifting your awareness of Self from a vantage point of 'half a step' behind your external ego-self. Here, you can observe yourself and others without getting emotionally entangled (and ineffective). Can you imagine easing up on your emotionally fused reactions and, instead, be the proactive force in your own life, independent of other people's actions, comments and opinions?

- ***By connecting with more than just your intellectual intelligence, you will have a wider and deeper place from where you can make your decisions.*** Decision-making requires far more than just your intellectual intelligence. Great leaders are physically intelligent and emotionally intelligent as well. They know how to read a room, read emotions, and use their body and voice in a way that behooves the situation in front of them. Can you imagine being intelligent even in situations you now dismiss as impossible?

- ***By connecting with yourself, you learn to set boundaries around what you are capable of handling.*** Many leaders fall in the trap of being everything to everyone. All the while, they forget to be number one for themselves. All egos aside, you really do need to take care of yourself to make any positive impact in the world. Can you imagine being in touch with what you need, when you need it and having the guts to make space for that?

"I Don't Have Time"

Getting to a sparkie-flowy space when you're feeling stuck in a rut, tired and out of time is like looking at luxury chateaus on the Cote'd'Azur with 30 bucks in the bank. It is so far fetched and obviously not ever going to work. But you're a smart cookie, so start thinking about this wisely.

Most people I coach or talk to complain about *time* as the number one huge prison-wall hurdle to overcome (which they've already labeled impossible) before doing any kind of inner business work. Whatever you decide is true will be true, so if you really don't want to make a prison-break from suffering and feel that blaming your lack of time is your best bet, then by all means, your inner business will remain safely undeveloped.

For others, here's some good news:

Firstly: all we have is time. Use your problem solving abilities and make it work. If you, while doing one thing, fret over the next twelve things on your schedule today, of course you'll feel as if the time puzzle is impossible to solve. Once you get over that mind-block, you will open up to solutions. You're not a victim here. You have set your own life up. Remember how life is happening *for* you? So you put the big-kid panties on and make time work for you. Here's the truth: You have the right to make your time schedule work. If it doesn't work, you have the right to change it. You have enough love for you to ask others for help and you will make it work.

Anyone who thinks they don't have time to meditate can consider this: The more I meditate, the less sleep I need. The more I meditate, the more focused I become, and the fewer mistakes I make. The more I meditate, the more energetic I feel. The time savings are huge! Can you imagine how much time you would save from the lesser sleep needed and the time saved from avoiding unnecessary mistakes (and their subsequent cleanups) and from not being so slow and listless? It's sort of a "bet 1 get 4" kind of deal.

But the good news gets better. Here's for a deeper level.

Business often gets a bad rap as some necessary evil and something we wish we didn't have to be a part of. Truth be told, however, we are so lucky to be in business! We are heavenly blessed to have a job! Great fortune is bestowed upon us that we need to go to work! And before I go too far in what sounds like poetic delusion, here is my simple point: We need to make a living to support our families, so we need to decide how.

All of a sudden, from a short train of thought, based on our survival and business needs, we are in dialog with ourselves with one of the most profound questions in life. *Why Am I Here?*

So here we are, with a deep philosophical question about life—and we got it for free! Just by needing a job! We could have been born with silver spoons coming out a little here and there, with no real demands coming our way except the difficult choice between St Barts or The Hamptons for the week-end. But we're not! We get to deal with life's profound question.

And that's how we are lucky, blessed and fortunate.

Perhaps you chose a job and chased a career without consciously asking yourself the question *Why Am I Here?*

If so, you most certainly aren't alone.

Perhaps you are among a scary-large group of North Americans who are miserable in how they're spending their days. Good thing then that it's not too late to have a life and a job that you find meaningful and awesome. Which, surprisingly, doesn't have to mean that you get a new job. As per our mindfulness pointers, *wherever you go, there you are.*

Wherever you are in your work situation,
asking yourself why you are here will be a fruitful
continuation of your job journey,
wherever that may be.

We may be having this dialog just as you are transitioning from having a job to pursuing a career, or from having a career to finding your vocation. You may finally find the answer to why you have chosen the job you already have and be happy with that. Or you may pull the big red brake and say *Hell No, I'm getting off this train.*

Wherever you come from and wherever you think you are heading, you probably have many thoughts and feelings about your job already. Perhaps a few hundred of these thoughts repeat themselves every day, and your feelings tag along with them. And then you're wondering why you're exhausted…

When we go to work we go and *do* something. That's our job. Whether it is thinking about how to best divide an atom or helping old ladies go to the bathroom with dignity, we are doing something.

And you have chosen leadership on some level, which means that you are leading not just yourself in doing something but you are also trying to lead other people's doing. That amounts to a lot of doing. So, beyond the mechanics of your job, what are you doing? What is the core of your doing? What resonates with your meaningful contribution to this place? *Why are you here?*

Rhetorically, if I ask you *Are you here to help other people feel really bad about themselves?* – I'd readily assume that your answer is "no." If we are asked *Are you here to experience as little joy as possible? Are you here to suffer as much as possible?* We say these are silly questions, the answer is no and no!

Our actions in reality, however, answer differently. If we're being honest with ourselves, we actually *don't* make it a priority to make ourselves and people around us feel good. We *don't* prioritize joy. We *should* be able to stand a great deal of suffering and sacrifice because of our bigger paychecks or because life is just plain hard, right?

If you feel that it's hard to find an answer to why you are here, your experiences so far can give you valuable clues. You have done enough of what you enjoy and don't enjoy to have certain preferences. If you can tune in with your preferences and weed out the ones that don't resonate with your sense of spark, you have some answers right there.

The reason that we want to go beyond the expectations that have been put on us (by others and ourselves) and even go beyond our own programming, is that expectations and programming come from other people. Not from you. You are now exploring the depths of why *you* are here, not why someone else thinks you're here. Those answers could readily be watered down to "provide for the family", "climb as far as possible on the power ladder", "collect as much monetary assets for coming generations before I die as possible" type uninspiring answers. You can provide for your family all you want, in fact, I'm proud to provide for mine. But I don't confuse that with the much deeper question of why I am here, what my contribution to the world is.

We need to start a deeper dialog with ourselves
in order to create a life we are interested in.

There are no right or wrong answers when you are trying to get to the core of why you are here and who you are.

Since "Why am I here" is one of the most profound questions in life, we want to keep an open mind, an open heart and be in touch with our souls. Yup. And if the question seems too severe or if you're drawing a blank, there are variations of it that may resonate better with you, such as:

- What can I do, that I would love to do, to contribute to a better world? Or,
- Through whatever I am actually doing, what is the common thread that brings me joy?
- How can I serve a greater good while also being good to myself?

See your truthful answers as your own guiding stars in your life. Then the marriage between Doing (action) and Purpose (meaning) will happen all by itself.

When I was 5 years old, my mother always told me that happiness was the key to life. When I went to school, they asked me what I wanted to be when I grew up. I wrote "happy". They told me I didn't understand the assignment, and I told them they didn't understand life.
–John Lennon

100% More Intelligent

As I have alluded to before, the source of our intelligence is not singular. We are pretty much indoctrinated to think about intelligence as a closed off area of ourselves called our intellect. This is primarily our left brain hemisphere, the place where logic and reason rule. Just looking at our brains a little closer, and especially how the brain is reacting to different stimuli and what works in life, it is evident that our intelligence is much more than logic.

Body

Our bodies, as an example, are a great source of intelligence. In scientific studies, they have measured situations where the body knows information before the brain. In these studies, the body has also been more accurate at guessing things that neither the body nor the brain had any previous information about or could know. The body can react with sweaty palms as an example of signaling that it knows certain information before the brain has figured it out. I call this physical intelligence.

Many big leaders have a physical intelligence as their primary intelligence.

My dad is a very physically intelligent person. He has gone down in business history books for being a remarkably gutsy CEO. He built an empire by daring to acquire one construction company after another, all the while no one else dared to even buy a full tank of gas. He is a masterful mingle-guy, makes everyone feel seen and is very sensitive to a room. He is the same kind of person who has gotten out of several sure-death accidents by reacting logically the "wrong" way, but physically the only way that would save his life. His physical intelligence has and still is one of his greatest assets.

I know what it feels like in me when I use my physical intelligence. It feels like an informer of sorts, speaking to me through physical signals. My body is great at letting me know what I really feel and think about a situation or a person whereas my logic can be lost at hello. My body even tells me to avoid certain things, as if it is flagging for danger. Even as a problem solver, my hands figure things out way before my logic has grasped the situation.

It has taken me some experimentation before I have been able to trust the mechanics of this, but I have to say, it's pretty spot on nowadays. The more I have listened to my body, the more accurate information I seem to get. The sensation I get in the pit of my stomach as I conclude that I shouldn't trust someone is very specific. There are still times when I go against that very particular feeling and every time it turns out that the feeling was right. It also seems like this kind of physical intelligence is connected to certain things or to certain people. My body lifts up the phone before certain people call, but not others. I enjoy exploring this.

We all have a physical intelligence inside of us. As we connect to our physical bodies in an aware, present way, we can all start tapping in to the many layers of what this intelligence has to offer. If you start paying attention to your physical intelligence, you will discover some pretty crazy things, and not only relating to what you need in order to function and flourish, but also as it related to "tuning in" to what other people are feeling, as a form of physical communication. That gives you loads of new information to fold in to your decision making process.

Did you know, by the way, that there are so many nerve connections happening in our stomachs, our guts, that the stomach is coined our "second brain"? Add to that that most of our immune system resides in our stomachs, and all of a sudden this system we call our body becomes quite fascinating, even in the way we look at intelligence.

Heart

Another intelligence that I am personally very fascinated by, perhaps because it is not one that was prevalent in my upbringing, is the intelligence that resides in our hearts.

**I have found no other part of our intelligence
that is as wise as our hearts.**

The heart seems to love conversation. It is through the dialog between people and people's hearts that we can access this deep wisdom. It is my sneaking suspicion that women are (generally speaking) more prone to conversing, especially in pairs, as we are raised to think that it's more okay to be caring and emotional because we are women. In other words, our programming has given us permission to be more emotionally wise.

I am convinced that future leadership (starting now) demands a deep, wise intelligence to make this planet one we can continue calling our home.

I am also convinced that our heart intelligence has nothing to do with gender. I nevertheless find it interesting to observe that this wise intelligence has been dismissed as "emotional" just because it has been a female trait attached to it. But make no mistake: the heart is very, very strong.

Let's all make the heart intelligence gender neutral, otherwise we'll have a future body of leadership consisting mostly of women, which would bring way too much peace, awareness, maturity and sustainability to the business world. That would… Wait, what? Ehm, actually… I take it all back. Let's not mention this to anyone!

Soul

You know that feeling of being connected to other people, being able to vibe them in, have a sense of people and things that defies reason and even time? In my experience, there is a type of intelligence that is even beyond our logical intellect, informative bodies and wise hearts. I call it the soul intelligence. This is where intuition resides. It is the intelligence in us that can connect with all other beings' soul intelligence. This is where we feel like we have always known certain people, though we've never previously met. As far as our logic will have it.

Soul intelligence knows something else, sees other things and can make conclusions far off the beaten path of intelligence.

When you encounter people with whom you feel you have a soul-bond, don't let your logic talk you out of believing that it's true. When you deeply recognize that we are here to learn and grow, you will invite people who you resonate with, because they will either be great for you because they are awesome, or they will be great for you because you will grow from the lessons learned with them.

The more you trust your soul's intelligence, the less time you will waste on things that aren't fun or things that don't help you grow.

Intelligence Math

If you add your physical intelligence, your heart intelligence and your soul intelligence to the intelligence of your intellect, you'll be, round figures, 100% more intelligent. Maybe even more. This is based on convincing nonscientific evidence in the shape of my own life. You start your intelligence experiment coupled with a daily meditation practice and let me know how it goes for you. Deal?

It may feel weird to allow yourself to accept an expanded intelligence base working for you. Perhaps it's scary to "think" with all senses open and your imagination working top level. You may even feel that this "taking life in completely" would make it seem like you've been making embarrassingly poor decisions for yourself for so long that becomes too painful to admit.

Two things are infinite:
the universe and human stupidity;
and I'm not sure about the universe.
—Albert Einstein

If it's any consolation, I have discovered that by and large, there is not much we can do wrong. We may fear being perceived as stupid, but really, events just are. The events in your life are what lead you to this point, but they are not you.

What you may discover in your inquiry of what on earth you are doing on earth, is that you are currently running down a path in a direction where you actually don't want to go. Don't panic. It's okay. Keep in mind that choosing a new course is not to say that all that you have done so far has been a waste of time.

I saw an interview with actor Steve Martin once where he said that everything he has ever learned in life, no matter how mundane or silly, he has needed to know at some point in his acting career.

When I studied Fine Arts at a university in New York, I thought it would be appropriate to also study American History. Although I had always felt connected with the US from spending part of my upbringing in the States, I hadn't actually studied the nation's history in-depth. I felt excited about connecting even deeper.

As it turned out, all classes for American History were full. And don't ask me how it seemed like such a natural second choice, but I immediately thought, *then I'll take African History!* Living in New York City, I guess it just seemed close enough. Trust me, I am not oblivious to the fact that it sounds nuts. But what I am fascinated by is how such a weird but (to me at the time) *given* decision came to mean so much to my career.

When I landed my first big job as a Creative Director for a strategic communications agency in Los Angeles, I was appointed to creatively lead an African development project for a huge consortium. There I was in the boardrooms of serious business and knew not only what languages were spoken in the different countries in question but could carry conversations about the Benin art era and important historical and religious facts relevant to the project. Sure, I wouldn't have been able to name all of the American presidents, but that didn't matter.

What you do today, especially as you invite all your intelligences to weigh in, experiences that you have on the subway-ride back from work or your next softball game may very well be the turning keys for important opportunities ahead.

They may not "echo in eternity" as the Gladiator so dramatically put it in his inspirational pre-battle speech, but the little things you encounter, matter. Especially, I have found, when more guts than thoughts lead the way. There is a curious power in staying present. You are at least 100% more intelligent than you thought.

So stay alert, keep your mind calm as you take it all in—and watch with curiosity how everything becomes relevant.

How Am I A Creator?

I have talked to many business people that feel held back by their past decisions and the current burden of being the breadwinner for their family. Never going for a life of their dreams is excused with arguments such as, *"Well I could have been doing real top level stuff, but I didn't get in to the right college and so, I never really had the chance."* Or, *"I stayed too long at my past job, I was just too loyal and didn't develop with the market as much as I could have"*, not to mention *"I had my kids young and never had the chance"*.

The decision for these guys has already been made, based on ancient history. They are not gonna go for a life that makes them happy because there is proof as to why that won't happen. This is logic to them. In their minds, they have decided that only people who have gone to the top Ivy League schools have the contacts and opportunities to make the big huge dream come true. And now they're not part of this magic club and therefore have the license to feel sorry for themselves. *Phew! I have something to blame should anyone ever question the fruits of my career!*

This happens on many different levels with a few set blame variables; if it's not education or lack of funds, it's a disloyal business partner, race, gender, kids or our accents that get the blame.

What we seem to be forgetting when we try to find scapegoats for our misfortune and short comings is that…
…some of the most successful business people come from troublesome or humble backgrounds and
…blaming people or circumstance will help you with only one thing: continuing to be stuck.

> *Sometimes, in order to be happy in the present moment,*
> *you have to give up hope for a better past.*
> —Dr Robert Holden

When we're in blame mode, we are forgetting about some of the most influential business minds in the world such as Steve Jobs, Oprah Winfrey and Bill Gates. (Maybe you've heard of them?)

There are many wonderful examples of people who have followed their passions and contributed so greatly to the world while challenging the confines of business management. Yet they are living their dream, far off the charts of any Ivy League vision. I have already mentioned Richard Branson who puts entertainment first and business rules last. Many have heard of the unwilling billionaire who founded Patagonia, Yvon Chouinard, who also wrote the book *Let My People Go Surfing*.

With the blueprint of your unique soul, you are the architect, the contractor, the interior designer, the plumber and the janitor. Sounds like a lot of work, I know, but whether you do it consciously or not, you're already doing it. So if you're not doing it, it means it's not getting done. Or you may be doing it poorly, with the same results. So, for good for bad, no one else can do the work for you because it's your life! Which means that you can also be the demolisher or the administrative stick in the wheel that will make sure to find a reason why the project will *never* be done so help you god. Your life, your choice.

When you come to a fork in the road, take it.
—Yogi Berra

You already have all the resources within reach to have the kind of job you want and become the kind of leader you want to be. And you won't find them anywhere but inside yourself.

There are no real excuses for not living the life that you dream of. Your excuses, on the other hand, are fantastic if you want to be held back, if you don't have the guts to be living your dream, and if you're afraid that your brother will be jealous if you do. Seriously, jealousy from family and friends is a huge unconscious factor why many people put a lid on themselves. The cost of not being accepted by our community if we shine too much or have it too good is too scary to even contemplate.

So let's break it down: if you, as a starting off point, shine with success based on your true self and not your ego, your success will not make you a flaunting diva. You will feel real. Other people will feel your meaningful contribution and heart of service. They will wish you well and be as supportive as ever. If you have taken that step within yourself, there is no reason for you to continue counting on the support from your family and so called friends if they are still jealous and small-minded. This is how you need to be a loving protector of your own potential, which may entail getting new friends or even a new family.

There may even be genuinely valid reasons to not pursue your dream. You may not want to go for the big promotion with lots of travel because you're afraid that time apart from your kids will make your whole family suffer from your absence. That simply means that you have envisioned the wrong dream. If your true dream involves spending quality time every day with your kids, don't forget to include that in your dream! It would be so silly to waste your life living someone else's dream.

**Your dream is your dream. And you are the one
that will make it happen. Not by just doing,
but by being what you are dreaming for.**

It's easy to be observant of the obvious necessity of "being what you dream for" when you get seated next to a sarcastic, loud and obnoxious person who is honestly surprised not to have found a mate yet that is honest, easy-going and pleasant. The person is being the opposite of what he or she is wanting to attract in his or her life. Good luck with that, we say.

The same truth is applicable to how we dream our dreams and create our lives. As the sole directors of how we choose to respond the events of our lives, all eyes are on us. Are we complaining and making excuses? Yes we are. So let's become honest and clear with our dreams, find inspiring alternatives for our excuses and start living our dream already.

Everything you say and do that keeps you identified with past PMS (poor me syndrome) experiences need to go, no matter how much you have used them as an excuse for not taking responsibility for your own happiness and success. Thank you. Bye bye.

These past experiences that you keep judging as bad or unfortunate or evil or great are in fact just past experiences. The moment you can let them just be - that they just "are", minus the adjectives - you will give yourself the space to move on towards the life you dare to imagine. And I mean dare. Because what you imagine will eventually be. So how gutsy are you?

Imagination Train

Honestly, who needs a gravy train when we all have access to an imagination train? Our imagination is so much more than making up nifty children's stories and believable excuses for our accountants. Our imagination holds tremendous power. Think about it! Everything that exists today was once only someone's imagination. That includes you and the Brooklyn Bridge. It's quite mind blowing!

What is now proved was once only imagined.
—William Blake

If everything that you call "real" today started as a seed and grew to a clear vision in someone's imagination, what will you imagine now? What are you currently thinking and feeling in to existence?

Take a moment and really imagine in your minds eye what it is you want to have materialized or happen in your life. Close your eyes and spend a few minutes to really experiencing the scene that you intend to have in your life. Use as many senses as you can in your scene. Really feel that you are there, showing up in the way that you wish for. Play the scene out and, as you exit the scene in your minds eye, before you open your eyes, make sure to connect your scene with your belief that this is what you now invite in your life. "I invite this truth, or something better, for the greater good of all, in my life. Every step I take from here on out is helping materialize the scene that already exists". Then open your eyes.

I like to add on the "or something better" since I realize that there's a limitation to the greatness I can dream up. I get a little Swedish about it and do the whole "who am I to…" thing. This way I know that no greatness is left behind.

Imagination is more important than knowledge.
For knowledge is limited to all we now know and understand,
while imagination embraces the entire world, and all there ever
will be to know and understand.
—Albert Einstein

Your Ticket To Ride

As you are standing on the platform of self-connection and meaningful contribution, your ticket to get on the imagination train and find your true spark is to practice kindness. There is nothing more important in spark than to be kind. Kindness starts in you for you. It grows out from your being of kindness to actions of kindness.

With kindness, the circle of spark is complete.

It's easy to get discouraged by all the unkindness and violence going on the world, even at our own offices. But know that kindness is light and will always, no matter what, outshine darkness. I don't mean to sound too religious about it, but we really are light on the inside. We really are kindness on the inside – and we can choose to connect with this.

With kindness, you are bypassing your ego, skipping energy-draining battles and are, effectively, creating a super highway to your spark.

I know several coined geniuses that are known as far from pleasant people. Don't let their weakness of lacking kindness be an inspiration to you. No level of genius is an excuse for being an ass. If someone is not kind to others, they are sure to be unkind with themselves. Not only do they invite a miserable internal life and an unfulfilled potential of joy, they are doing themselves the biggest disservice of all; they are not allowing themselves to truly live life. As they don't nurture themselves on the inside, they are also (both metaphorically and sometimes literally) killing themselves.

Brain Switching

The more I read about the brain and how it connects to genius, the more I realize that there are super genius regions in all of our brains. The only question is how we connect with these regions. Some are born with brain "deficiencies" or get injured in life, which allows for full-on access to this super genius brain with which we are all born. For the rest of us, without these genius-promoting injuries, we are left with finding ways to accessing these regions with some good ol' trickery.

Without any academic degree on the subject matter, I have still observed, studied and learned quite a few things about the workings of our brain connected to human performance. Through my years as a Creative Director and as a CEO, I have seen that, in addition to expanding our intelligence to include all our intelligences, it is our ability to switch *how* we're using our brains that makes the genius difference.

Everyone I have worked with, including myself, seems to find the best creative, innovative and genius heights when they switch with ease between our left (calculated) brain hemisphere and our right (creative) hemisphere. Remember, we have already examined our expanded notion of intelligence and the power of our imagination. Now, let's have our brains work top-shelf for us. As I have learned more and more about the brain, the pieces of my experience in the workplace have fallen in to place.

One thing I have observed is that people who have chugged along with their analytical abilities and just thought deeper and harder about a challenge in front of them, have not seemed to come at all as far as those who have been mixing in play or fun. Initially, this made very little sense to me, and it puzzled me for a long time. How can partial monkeying around make a difference? How can even meditation make a difference?

The more I've read up on neuroscience (and the further this surprisingly "new" field comes along), the clearer it is that any activity that puts you in the deep creative presence of your right brain, will inform your intellectual endeavors on your left side. In other words, monkeying around or meditating can activate the brain's right regions enough to help the intellectual and calculated left side.

Seeing how the intellectual businessman would benefit from meditation and art classes actually made sense pretty quickly. I think we've all seen wonders happen to brainy people who have loosened up a little.

A big nut for me to crack as a CEO however was to understand why my so-called creative people suddenly weren't creative. If you, like me, make your money off of good ideas, creating anything artistic or rely on innovation and new thinking for your bottom-line, I'm sure you can relate.

I like to experiment, which is always a great idea if you can admit that you're wrong (the experiment didn't work) and try something new. When I realized that a brain-hemisphere-exchange could do wonders for an expanded use of the brain, I wanted to try to up the level with my Creatives. Short of giving them algebra exercises to jog up their left brains, I asked them to have a structured awareness of the budget of the projects they were working on. It made sense from a "left brain supporting the right brain" perspective. But that didn't help. In fact, it backfired.

What I concluded from my observations and experiments is that the brain hemisphere switching was still the solution, but that the mistake Creatives often make is that they try to be creative from their *calculated mind*, not their creative present mind. I.e. they were trying to be creative from the left side of the brain that thinks too much to be present. (Duh!) In that space, they are worrying about the outcome, they are constantly judging their own performance, they are comparing themselves to past experiences and to the accomplishment of other Creatives.

I'm sure you can relate to this with your innovative qualities and those of your staff. We get stuck in a creative rut. And we used to be so good! But all we really need is to use both sides of the brain and keep in mind that our left side is usually way over-stimulated. We need our right! If we aren't present, we effectively can't connect with spark and hence start to underperform as creative people. Shucks. That leads us right back to kindness.

(You didn't see that one coming, did you?).

The Precious Present

You see, true kindness actually requires presence and, as such, will activate the right side of your brain (your new BFF). Presence is the root to all your leadership greatness, and that's why kindness is such a great ticket. Aside from the obvious benefit of being a great person.

And if you're wondering what kindness has to do with presence, think of it this way: It is only in presence that you can see or sense what the situation requires in order for you to contribute with kindness. You cannot be kind if you are not present. Again, kindness is about you in relation to you, to people you meet, to your company and to the world.

As you do, who knows, you may even realize that there is no real difference between you and them. In other words, that how you treat yourself is how you treat others. How others treat you may not be your business, but certainly how you react. You are the epicenter of your own experience. You may even feel that what's going on in the world is a reflection of how we are all thinking and that the symptomatic evil that we witness "out there" has its root cause "in here". Thankfully, you can change you.

You can't be kind on autopilot, neither to yourself nor to others, as non-presence will soon make you miss your kind mark. Besides, kind actions towards one person are not necessarily considered kind to another. That's why kindness requires tuning in.

Kindness is in presence itself and
kind actions arise from that presence.

You observe someone hurrying towards the elevator you're in, just as the doors are closing. In presence, you are kind enough to stop the doors from closing and welcome the person in. The simple act of holding up the door for someone requires you to be there, aware. Just like when you offer your colleague sugar snaps, you are better off if you remember that she is diabetic. Oops. If you're not present, you can't really help.

There are many more complex situations in your life that require more of your presence and total awareness in order to handle them well. It can certainly sound oxymoronic to be a kind leader, because we have this idea that leaders have to make tough decisions and be badass about it. But being a leader and being kind don't have to be conflicting notions. The kindest thing to do as a leader, as an example, can be to let someone go. That's not the first thing you think about when someone gets fired, but it really can be the truth. Others may initially look at you as a cruel bastard, but truth be known, if you consistently connect with your kindness as you make necessary decisions for the company, people will catch on to that. Once you connect with kindness and your acts emanate from kindness (both to yourself, to others, to the company and to the world), you will have people and events flow around you like a sweet stream.

> *Kindness is the language that the blind can see*
> *and the deaf can hear.*
> —Mark Twain

Kindness is easy to give to the kind. The sign of a truly great leader is someone who can be kind to the unkind and still feel safe in his or her own boat.

Idiots, Kindness And Clarity

Time and again, kind people are portrayed as idiots in movies. We apparently love to tell stories how one dumb sucker after another trusted someone too much or loved someone too much, and—as a result—became even bigger idiot losers. I really wonder why we equate kindness with stupidity. So, just to be clear: When I'm suggesting that you be kind, I'm not suggesting that you be an idiot.

> **Of all the traits out there, kindness is one of the sharpest**
> **choices you can make in your career.**

Be kind to everyone, even (or especially) the unkind. You can at least try. Leave every relationship—be it with business partners, contractors, lovers or housekeepers—as peaceful as you can. Be the one that lets go of being right without flaunting the fact that you just took the high-road. You know who you are anyway. As you make decisions for the company, really feel what the affected parties feel, connect with your kindness. You'd be a short-sighted dummy if you didn't.

Here's another version of the same truth to be considered: You won't get screwed just because you're nice. You get screwed when you are nice for the wrong reasons or if you don't have any integrity. Any wrong reason for being nice comes from being scared. A lot of people mask their fear with an image of being kind. We can make a whole long list of different scenarios of "nice" decisions based on fear. They will range from being afraid of being disliked, of confrontation, of being wrong, or it may even be a little more complex as you find yourself caught in a web where you feel you have to make super nice decisions regarding someone who could easily tell on you or cancel favors if you don't continue with your bought kindness. Whatever this list is, it's all based on kindness from fear. That is not kindness. If you are being a scared push-over, please stop calling yourself kind. You're scared. And that's okay. Go deal with it.

A downside I have experienced of being genuinely kind is that people are programmed to only believe urgencies that come with a level of aggression. With that programming, there's a risk that people will not take your kind instructions seriously. Being extraordinarily clear with your expectations will remedy that. I have found, especially as a kind woman dealing with "manly men", that I have to be exceptionally clear on every action-point, every time frame, and any consequence to them should they not meet the instructions. I don't want to be yelling and be rude. And I don't have to. But I have to be skilled at being clear.

Mindfulness Attitude: Beginner's Mind

A beginner's mind is a mind that is awake. It's as if it sees everything for the first and last time, not dismissing it as something it already knows or as something that prepares it for the next step. It is an open curiosity of the here and now.

Without an awakened curiosity about life, you will never be great at developing extraordinary business.

Spark is the fruit of a beginner's mind. Having this attitude opens up for innovation and creativity. This makes no sense to Mr. Ego. He is used to ruffling his feathers and using his fixed mind as a self-proclaimed expert to justify his high fees. But here's the deal: your value does not come from knowing it all. Your value comes from applying your open curiosity to your experience. Make it a habit to listen and ask questions, and your beginner's mind will start working for you.

In the beginner's mind there are many possibilities,
but in the expert's there are few.
—Shunryu Suzuki

There is much more power behind this attitude than what might first meet the eye.

If you actually manage to live in a state of curiosity—of being awake and open to seeing the world anew and being surprised—you will learn things and see things you never saw and never dared to dream of. My bet is that you'll start having a lot more fun as well.

A mind that thinks it knows it all has nothing left to learn, nothing left to see and cannot create. It is the kiss of death to spark. Without curiosity you grow complacent. Your imagination grows rusty.

The way life has given me great returns on being curious extends far beyond my creative capacity and scientific "testing-everything" drive. Time and again, my beginner's mind turns seemingly "bad" situations around to revealing great possibilities. How could it not? When I see the world anew, new solutions appear. As this state of mind matures, nothing "bad" can ever really happen, as events just are. This makes for a rich and free life.

Begin folding this attitude of cultivating a beginner's mind into your life and feel the excitement of not knowing everything. With this attitude, notice how new ideas are presented to you. Practice noticing your own sense of what it means to have a beginner's mind. This is you seeing the world for you. See new things where you did not pay attention before. Especially practice seeing something new in what your mind already has decided that it knows.

I always thought my dad was a very square businessman. Growing up, I wrote him off as a senior white male type leader that relied on logic alone. It wasn't until later in my life, as our CEO conversations became deeper and more meaningful, that I understood that he used a beginner's mind far more often than I had seen fit the picture. I used to probe him on what constitutes his decision-making, but he never really admitted that intuition had anything to do with it. It turns out, however, that unbeknownst to him, he had some really good spark tricks going.

In the early years of his career, he worked as a Planning Engineer, a completely new role at a construction site at the time. As a means to constantly improve results at work, he implemented a rule for himself to come up with one completely new idea every day. This way, he challenged himself to never grow complacent while assuring that, to the best of his ability, the job was done with the best solutions possible. Or in his own words "I didn't give up until I had found at least one completely new solution every day. It took time, which was good, because then I didn't have to participate in the B.S. downtime talk going on between the men". Twenty-five years later, he was the global CEO of the same company. Coincidence? I think not. I wonder what the B.S. downtime talkers talk about today.

What can you vow to see differently at your job? What can you put in place, with a beginner's mind, that will make new solutions appear? How about your view of yourself; what haven't you seen in yourself in a long time? What would you see if you saw your spouse as if for the first time? How about your employees or your ride to work or your business expansion plan? What if you took nothing for granted?

> *Yesterday I was clever, so I wanted to change the world.*
> *Today I am wise, so I am changing myself.*
> —Rumi

Mindfulness Attitude: Gratitude

You are still here; your heart is beating, most parts of you are still functioning, you have a mind, you are in life, the sun is shining and warms you. These are wonders worth your sincere gratitude. The more you connect with your sense of gratitude, the more you are inviting yourself into the present moment, and the more you invite situations for which to be grateful. This is a wheel of giving and receiving gratitude that ultimately connects you with a true sense of happiness. This is a spark-promoting machine!

> *The miracle of gratitude is that*
> *it shifts your perception to such an extent*
> *that it changes the world you see.*
> —Dr Robert Holden

Previously at Harvard University, Shawn Achor is a best-selling author on the subject of happiness and how it relates to a better life and better business. Amongst the highlights of his research is the simple truth that happiness is a choice and that happiness is connected to meaningful contribution.

Achor is joining quite a few people before him who have gathered evidence that gratitude invites more good things in life. And it really makes sense, doesn't it? If you keep looking for things to be grateful for, that's the stuff you'll start noticing more.

If you take a couple of minutes each day, and single out the details from the last 24 hours for which you can be grateful, think about them, savor them and write them down, you are effectively reliving the positive experience. A visualization and an actual experience makes no real difference for the brain, so by reliving the detailed highlights of your day, you will not only feel pleasant from reliving it, but it has proven to give greater life satisfaction and meaning. Time to get a gratitude journal!

Based on convincing research data, Achor has another great project you can undertake to get more greatness start flowing in to your life. He recommends that you take two minutes each morning for 21 days to communicate appreciation or a thank you to someone in your support network – it can be a coworker, friend, mentor, family member and it can be done face-to-face, over the phone or as an email. When you extend this praise and thank you to 21 different people, you will practice how to give praise without any buts and ifs. (Let's skip the "you're so awesome, but" and "you're great, if it wasn't for").

The extraordinary benefit of this 21-day gratitude project, is that you will not only feel happier as you do it, you will deepen the quality of your social connections and relationships, with the turbo bonus of a longer life. As it turns out, the quality of our social network is a predictor of our longevity, more so than smoking is to cancer or obesity is to high blood pressure.

21 days, praise 21 people, be happier, live longer, backed up by Harvard. You just gotta know a good deal when it's staring at you.

Mindfulness Attitude: Generosity

There is great joy and satisfaction in cultivating an attitude of generosity. As you grow increasingly attentive towards your own presence in life, you can easily give of yourself to bring others joy. As you experience the power of giving yourself to life, you are fully immersing yourself in the interconnection with other people. There is no other way to successfully run your life—or a company—because without interconnectivity, you really don't have anything.

It's so easy to make the mistaken math that the more money you gain and the harder you hold on to it, the more money you'll have. But money is energy, and it doesn't work that way. It needs to move, or it becomes stagnant. We cannot accumulate money as energy and think that it will be a set piece of asset.

Have you ever noticed, that when you smile at people and feel friendly towards them, you get more smiles and experience more friendliness? That's an emotional and attitudinal what-goes-around-comes-around type deal. That's how we are interconnected. As you are smiling, you are not primarily smiling to get a smile back. What you *are* is happy and it costs you nothing to be friendly. You have clicked in with happiness on the inside of you, and now you are simply sharing yourself. You feel much happier by giving of your joy.

You can think of money in the same way. *What?? I'm not freely giving my money away to strangers!!* I know, and that's cool (although, between taxes, bad business deals and charitable contributions, you kind of already are). But here's the thing: You never make money in isolation. Any business is a form of exchange, and my point is that it is through being a catalyst for the wheel of exchange that you make it spin and grow. Remember how nothing happens until something moves? That's a great way to connect money with generosity.

Beyond monetary gains, generosity really does have to do with experiencing the joy of giving. You are not separate. As you give, you receive.

> *Be generous in all areas of your life.*
> *The more you give of yourself and all that flows to you,*
> *the more you'll see flowing back to you.*
> —Dr. Wayne Dyer

Generosity is where so many of mindfulness' attitudes come together. Generosity makes you **accept**, in the depths of you, that you are not separate from others. As you give to others, you give to yourself and **non-judging** becomes second nature.

With **patience**, you will give without demanding any immediate return. Life will show you the ripple effects of your generosity, in time. You will **trust** that your giving is always giving well spent.

As you **consciously strive** for a better life for you and for everyone else, your generosity will play a natural part of moving forward and making a difference.

With a **beginner's mind**, perhaps you can find new ways of showing your staff that you are grateful to them for being loyal and doing the job so well. Implementing random acts of kindness with your staff will be one of many joyous examples you can come up with.

With an attitude of **letting go**, give yourself to the flow of sharing. Share your stories, share your memories, share your laughs, share your advice, share your vulnerability, share your heart, share your strength, and share your life. Hey, you might even want to share your avocado.

In this space, you will know for sure, that there is no better gift than giving.

The Briefing on SPARK

- When you cultivate spark, the world won't be able to get enough of you.

- Having spark means living in-spirit, where living and sharing an inspired life is not only what you do, but who you are.

- Anyone can develop spark.
    - If you know how to connect with yourself,
    - If you are passionate about making a meaningful difference,
    - If you get on the imagination train,
    - If you practice kindness.

- If you start utilizing the intelligence of your body, heart and soul, in addition to your intellect, you will be approximately 100% more intelligent. True story.
    - Many leaders are physically intelligent,
    - No other intelligence is more wise than our hearts,
    - Our soul intelligence can see anything as it is connected to everything.

- A few notes on kindness:
    - Being kind does not equate being an idiot. In fact, kindness is one of the sharpest choices you can make in business.
    - Kindness helps you to be present and only in presence can you experience life + you'll have a pleasant time being kind = smart move.
    - Stop calling yourself kind if your "kind" actions are based on fear.

o   With real kindness, you are bypassing your ego, skipping energy-draining battles and are, effectively, creating a super highway to your spark.

- Creativity is accessed through presence. You really can't think up a good idea when you are worried about the outcome or comparing your efforts to previous merits. You are not creative. See yourself as a vessel for creativity instead, far beyond yourself – and some pretty great things will start to flow out of you.

- You don't need a gravy train. You were born with an imagination train! Your imagination holds tremendous power. Think about it: Everything that exists today was once only someone's imagination. That includes you and the Brooklyn Bridge.

- Contrary to popular belief, all we have is time. Use your smarts and make your time puzzle work for you. You created your life, remember?

- Everyone has genius regions in their brain. Most of us aren't trained at accessing them or have a brain "damage" that opens the gates to them. One genius trick us non-genius folks can try is to get skilled at brain-switching. For most of us, that would mean steering our brain activities over to the right side hemisphere more often—the expressive, the artistic, the joyous, the goal-less, the unmeasured, the present side—in order to enhance our left (strategic, logical) brain hemisphere and get turbo benefit from our brains.

- A great way to be totally uncreative and a terrible innovator is to be stressed out, overwhelmed, have no vision, refuse to admit to mistakes, distrust everything (especially life), and have no spark whatsoever. Sounds wonderful, right?

- Or, you can shine that light that is burning so bright inside you and share that with the world.

SPARK – Mind-Training Exercise

Mind-training:

Challenge yourself lovingly by doing something, in presence, that you normally don't do. Observe what you "always do" as per automation and see what happens when you change it.

Perhaps you want to try to fill out your gym membership application or your kid's next school form with your non-dominant hand? Or use your non-dominant hand for hair brushing, tooth brushing or wiping down the kitchen counter? Perhaps you can choose a different route to work every day for a whole week? Notice what you see. Choose the longest line in the super market on purpose. Notice how that feels. Let every car that wants to cut in front of you do so while feeling great about it. See what happens, both in you and with traffic. When you go back to your "normal" routines, note what you are discovering about yourself and your relationship to your "life as per usual".

SPARK – Meditation Practice

Last but not least on our joint meditation exploration, it is time for *informal* mindfulness meditation practice! This is a fun practice to incorporate to your everyday life that, like the rest of our meditation practices, will sharpen your ability to be present and focused. What I love about the informal exercises is that they bridge meditation into the normalcy of our lives.

Informal Mindfulness Meditation: 2-10 minutes

You can do the same informal practice every day, until you get to a sense of non-judgmental present moment awareness. If you feel urged to multi-task and your mind goes a mile a minute, come back to a focused awareness to the very task you have chosen. A play-by-play commentary to your exercises in your own head will not help you. Just observe that thoughts come up regarding the exercises and during the exercises, and let the thoughts just appear and disappear without paying any real attention to them.

Here are a few examples to choose from, something you can start incorporating today! This is really going to the mental gym as you are practicing with tasks you perform every day already, but now with the added practice of bringing your focus back to being completely present with the task at hand. This is a muscle you will benefit greatly from in other areas of your life where focus is required; a list that is long, to be sure.

- **Brushing your teeth.** Brush your teeth in full awareness, doing nothing but brushing your teeth, and not thinking about anything. Just observe the sensations of the brush meeting your teeth and gums. Observe the taste of the toothpaste in different parts of your mouth, hear the strokes, hear the water, smell the smells...

- **Doing the dishes.** Do your dishes in full presence, without thinking about anything else or wishing you were doing something else, just feel the sensations of the water. Listen to the dishes, to the bubbles, experience the fragrances, be aware of your body, movement, the textures of the dishes as they get clean...

- **Listening to a person.** When a person tells you something, listen to that person with full attention, without interrupting. No speaking, no agreeing, no opposing, no opinions, just listening. Make eye-contact and sense what happens in you as you are listening fully to someone else speak without any own agenda of comebacks or advice...

- **Taking the stairs.** Take the stairs in full presence, be aware of every step you take in the stairs. As your body moves from one step to another, notice how the weight of your body shifts, that the tension required from different muscles moves as your weight shifts. Be aware of your feet meeting the platform of each step and see if you can take one step without thinking about the next step or the end of the stairs...

- **Drinking tea.** Practice preparing and drinking tea (or coffee) in full awareness of the present moment. Join the process fully as the tealeaves blend with the hot water, your movements in the preparation, the smells, the sounds, the steam.... And the sensation as you lift the cup up, hand around the cup, cup touching your lips and the warm beverage in your mouth, slowly making its way down your throat, warming your chest...

- **Making the bed.** Immerse yourself in the presence of making your bed. Be fully there with your hands feeling the softness of your sheets, the strong movements of your muscles, the breeze from the sheets as they land on the bed, the scent, the sound of pillows, the different textures, your breathing...

When you have practiced one informal meditation (from above or one that you made up), for a few days straight, switch or add on another one. And then another. This is how life can become in constant meditation. Ah...

PART THREE

What now?

Your Friend

It is time for us to part. I want to thank you for allowing me to be your friend and guide as you have explored your inner business and all the awesomeness that you are.

And although you can always go back and re-read parts of this book that have hopefully felt like helpful hints, I want to remind you that you've got a friend in you.

Your friend is not sad when you cry. Your friend is not weak when you're feeling vulnerable. Your friend is not broken when you feel depressed. Your friend is resilient when you're struck by panic. Your friend has answers when you feel confused, and knows that you are the awesomeness of light and love when all you can see is darkness. Your friend is your awareness, your deep knowing and your deep truth.

Reconnect with your friend in your daily stillness. Start inviting this friend to your breakfast contemplations, business development sessions and board meetings. As you do, as I do, and as more of us do, we will indeed, through business, change the world in to something more beautiful than how we found it.

I look forward to connecting with you and your friend soon.

A truly good book teaches me better than to read it.
I must soon lay it down, and commence living on its hint.
What I began by reading, I must finish by acting.
—Henry David Thoreau

About The Author

Linda Björk, a.k.a. "The Meditating CEO," is a former Creative Director in Corporate America and a decade-long CEO of what she built to become one of Scandinavia's largest design and branding agencies. She is now dedicated to teaching meditation and mental skills to business leaders worldwide.

As an agency executive, Ms. Björk pioneered using meditation, mindfulness and mind-training to reach new, global levels with her staff. With her experience as a result-oriented CEO she is on a quest to change leadership in the world to embody awareness, grace and inclusiveness. Through speeches, executive coaching and her "inner business" focused corporate programs, Ms. Björk is guiding people from all walks of life to happiness, health and wealth. Clients include media executives, financial analysts, hospitality executives, creative directors and lawyers; even generals from The US Army and luxury fashion designers in NYC are recipients of Ms. Björk's unique meditation programs.

Ms. Björk lives in New York City with her daughter and has had a daily meditation practice of transcendental meditation (TM) since 1996. If she didn't inspire people to get their inner business in order, she claims she would be a comedian. No one thinks that's funny.